Therapeutic approaches in psychology

The use of psychological therapies to treat mental disorder is a key component of psychology courses at the introductory level. Susan Cave introduces the many therapies in use today, including cognitive-behavioural, humanistic and psychodynamic approaches. Their application to different mental disorders is discussed, as well as research methods in atypical psychology, the effectiveness of therapy, ethical issues and current practice.

Therapeutic Approaches in Psychology is tailor-made to the student new to higher-level study. It includes sections on methodology, community care and areas of more recent controversy such as the detrimental effects of therapy. With its helpful textbook features to assist in examination and learning techniques, it should interest all introductory psychology students as well as those training for the caring services.

Susan Cave is an Assistant Examiner and Coursework Moderator for A-level Psychology and a Lecturer in Psychology.

Routledge Modular Psychology

Series editors: Cara Flanagan is the Assessor for the Associated Examining Board (AEB) and an experienced A-Level author. Kevin Silber is Senior Lecturer in Psychology at Staffordshire University. Both are A-level examiners in the UK.

This *Routledge Modular Psychology* series is a completely new approach to introductory level psychology, tailor-made to the new modular style of teaching. Each short book covers a topic in more detail than any large textbook can whilst allowing teacher and student to select material exactly to suit any particular course or project.

The books have been written especially for those students new to higher-level study, whether in school, college or university. They include specially designed features to help with technique, such as a model essay at an average level with an examiner's comments to show how extra marks can be gained. The authors are all examiners and teachers at the introductory level.

The *Routledge Modular Psychology* texts are all user-friendly and accessible and include the following features:

- sample essays with specialist commentary to show how to achieve a higher grade
- chapter summaries to assist with revision
- progress and review exercises
- glossary of key terms
- summaries of key research
- further reading to stimulate ongoing study and research
- website addresses for additional information
- cross-referencing to other books in the series

Therapeutic approaches in psychology

Susan Cave

London and New York

First published 1999
by Routledge
11 New Fetter Lane, London EC4P 4EE

Simultaneously published in the USA and Canada
by Routledge
29 West 35th Street, New York, NY 10001

©1999 Susan Cave

Typeset in Times by Routledge
Printed and bound in Great Britain by Clays Ltd, St Ives PLC

British Library Cataloguing in Publication Data
A catalogue record for this book is available from the British Library

Library of Congress Cataloging in Publication Data
Cave, Susan, 1949–
Therapeutic approaches in psychology / Susan Cave.
(Routledge modular psychology)
Includes bibliographical references and index.
1. Psychotherapy.   I. Title.   II. Series.
RC480.C37   1999   98–45311
616.89'14–dc21   CIP

ISBN 0-415-18870-9 (hbk)
ISBN 0-415-18871-7 (pbk)

To Leigh, my husband and my best friend

'What we need are more kindly friends and fewer professionals'
(Masson 1988)

Contents

Illustrations

Figures

Tables

Preface

This book aims to convey the flavour and diversity of current psychological thinking, research and practice regarding the treatment of mental disorder. Primarily aimed at A-level and first year undergraduate students, it will be of equal interest to all those who care, as I do, about the everyday suffering induced by such disorders that is evident all around us.

The book attempts in the first chapter to introduce the reader to the different types of mental disorder, explanations (or 'models') for the disorders, and the varied range of therapeutic approaches. Each major type of therapeutic approach is then covered in a separate chapter (Chapters 2–6) in which the general principles are outlined, examples of therapies and their important techniques described, and the applicability of each therapy is discussed and illustrated with case studies or research. Later chapters deal with research into the effectiveness of therapies (Chapters 7 and 8), ethical issues associated with their use (Chapter 9), and with clinical practice (Chapter 10). The final chapter (Chapter 11) contains a selection of summarised key research papers, and sample student essays complete with examiner's comments.

Definitions of terms given in **bold** type in the text can be found in the Glossary, which begins on p. 151.

Acknowledgements

Thanks are long overdue to those who care, and are not afraid to make this plain in their writings and in their work. Science is a tool, and tools can always be used as weapons!

The series editors and Routledge acknowledge the expert help of Paul Humphreys, Examiner and Reviser for A-level Psychology, in compiling the Study Aids section of each book in this series.

They also acknowledge the Associated Examining Board (AEB) for granting permission to use their examination material. The AEB do not accept responsibility for the answers or examiner comment in the Study Aids section of this book or any other book in the series.

Introduction

Overview of the concept of abnormality
Classification of mental disorders
Models of mental disorder
Types of therapeutic approaches

Overview of the concept of abnormality

Who needs treatment?

Before we can begin to describe and evaluate the different types of treatment that are available for mental disorder, it is essential to consider first what exactly we mean by 'mental disorder' or 'abnormality'. Despite the fact that most cultures have acknowledged the existence of mental problems in some form, there are considerable discrepancies between cultures regarding what is considered to be unacceptable behaviour. The Yoruba of Nigeria, for example, are much less likely than the average American to consider that someone showing the symptoms of paranoid schizophrenia is mentally ill (Erinosho and Ayonrinde 1981). What is unacceptable can also change within a society over time, as can be seen in the case of homosexuality (which used to be classed as a mental illness). In an attempt to standardise the way that societies respond to such individuals, and to remove any possible subjective bias that a particular clinician might have, efforts have been made to draw up criteria which will provide an agreed definition of abnormality. The legal and social consequences for an individual categorised as abnormal are considerable, ranging from compulsory treatment and loss of freedom to social rejection. Therefore it is essential to develop criteria that can be universally and unambiguously applied.[1]

Criteria for defining abnormal behaviour

Abnormal behaviour has been defined using five different sets of criteria:

- *statistical criteria* define it as deviation from the average
- *deviation-from-the-norm criteria* define it as deviation from expected ways of behaving
- *mental health criteria* define it as the absence of socially desirable characteristics and behaviours (Jahoda 1958)
- *social/psychological criteria* define it by the presence of undesirable behaviours (Rosenhan and Seligman 1984)
- *mental illness criteria* define it by the presence of clusters of symptoms

This last approach is the most commonly used, and will be discussed further here. The clusters of behavioural symptoms identified are thought to indicate the presence of an underlying mental illness which may respond to treatment. For example, the most commonly used classification system at the moment is **DSM IV**, which defines mental disorder as:

> a clinically significant behaviour or psychological syndrome or pattern that occurs in a person and that is associated with present distress (a painful symptom), disability (impairment of one or more important areas of functioning), a significantly increased risk of suffering death, pain, disability, or an important loss of freedom. In addition, this syndrome or pattern must

---

1 See *Psychopathology* in this series for a detailed discussion of these issues.

not be merely an expectable response to a particular event such as, for example, the death of a loved one

(Gross and McIlveen, 1996)

To give an example, clinical depression would be defined by experiencing a low mood for at least two weeks, plus at least five of the following symptoms: change in appetite or weight; changes in sleep patterns; loss of energy; agitation or slowing down; loss of pleasure; guilt feelings; loss of concentration; suicidal thoughts. This system has its faults – for example, the assumption of a physical illness underlying the problem behaviours has been questioned, as has the reliability of the classification system. In practice, an eclectic approach that draws on a range of the criteria mentioned may well be the best compromise.

Taking each set of criteria for abnormality in turn, draw up a summary table to show what the criteria are, and see if you can think of any examples to show how they could be applied. Can you think of any difficulties that might be associated with each approach?

Progress exercise

Classification of mental disorders

When it comes to the classification of mental disorders, it may quite reasonably be expected that different therapies will be suited to different disorders. Thus it is essential to establish a reliable and valid classification system at the outset, so that we can identify a disorder and then prescribe a suitable treatment. As mentioned in the previous section, the most widely used system at present is DSM IV, which is an American system, and employs the categories detailed in Table 1.1. The system also suggests that each individual can be assessed on five axes of functioning (although only the first three are compulsory). As well as the syndromes outlined (see Table 1.1), these axes include medical, social, occupational and environmental influences on functioning.

Table 1.1 Major categories of mental disorder listed in DSM IV

Clinical disorders	Personality disorders
schizophrenia and other psychotic disorders	antisocial personality
mood disorders	paranoid personality
anxiety disorders	schizoid personality
somatoform disorders	schizotypal personality
dissociative disorders	borderline personality
factitious disorders	narcissistic personality
sex/gender disorders	avoidant personality
eating disorders	dependent personality
impulse control disorders	obsessive-compulsive personality
adjustment disorders	
disorders of childhood and adolescence	
cognitive disorders (e.g. dementia, amnesia)	
substance-related disorders	
sleep disorders	

As mentioned above, one of the main purposes of having a classification system is to establish categories of disorder which have common origins and will benefit from the same treatment. In practice, however, this has not proved to be so simple, and both the **reliability** and **validity** of the present systems have been questioned. Regarding reliability, several studies (e.g. Zigler and Phillips 1961) have found agreement between clinicians to be as low as 54 to 84 per cent. More recent research suggests that this figure may have improved, but given that subjective judgement is still required during the diagnostic process it is unlikely that agreement will become a great deal higher. When validity is considered, many categories (e.g. schizophrenia) contain individuals who appear to differ widely from one another in their behaviour, and do not respond to the same kinds of treatment. Other categories such as the anxiety disorders do not appear to have any common origins, and respond to a variety of treatments. As we shall see in later chapters, issues such as these make it very difficult to evaluate the effectiveness of treatments, or even to make treatment decisions in the first place.

Models of mental disorder

In the present context a 'model' means a view, or system of beliefs, about what causes mental disorders. Within psychology in general there are several different schools of thought, such as the behaviourist school and the psychodynamic or Freudian school, which offer competing explanations for most forms of behaviour.[2] Given the complexity of human behaviour, it is quite likely that several different views will be valid, even if one is more useful in a particular case. The same is true of mental disorders, but the models can be particularly influential in this area because not only do they offer competing explanations, they also suggest that different types of treatment will be suitable. We will expand on this in the next section.

Historically, the main conflict has been between the religious and the medical approaches to mental disorder. For example, in the Middle Ages the religious movements of the time were responsible for many abnormal individuals being regarded as victims of demonic possession who were consequently burnt at the stake. Physicians, however, still adhered to the view of Hippocrates in the fourth century BC, who held that the origins of such problems were medical. It was not until the early part of the nineteenth century that the terms 'madness' and 'lunacy' began to be replaced by the term 'mental disease'. 'Lunatics' became 'patients', and the asylum system became medicalised, aiming to cure rather than simply to confine. The *medical* (or *biomedical*) model was therefore the first of the modern approaches to emerge. The main assumption of this model is that the behavioural symptoms of mental illness reflect an underlying disease process, in the same way that the symptoms of a physical illness do. The model is supported by three kinds of evidence: research into the effects of brain damage on behaviour; research into genetic influences on behaviour; and research into the links between abnormal behaviour and disordered communication systems in the nervous system. An example of the first type of research is given in the case of Phineas Gage, outlined in Case study 1.1.

2   A detailed account of these is given in *Psychopathology* in this series.

Case study 1.1: Phineas Gage

Phineas Gage was a railway worker who suffered brain damage when a piece of metal 3 feet 7 inches long and 1 inch in diameter was propelled into his skull by an explosion. The rod entered his left cheek and came out through the top of his skull. His motor and sensory functions and general physical health were unchanged after the accident, but his behaviour was so different that he was no longer considered employable. The main change was that he became less restrained, that is 'he is fitful, irreverent, indulging at times in the grossest profanity....manifesting but little deference for his fellows, impatient of restraint or advice when it conflicts with his desires...devising many plans for future operations which are no sooner arranged than they are abandoned' (Harlow 1868: 339–40).

The *psychodynamic model*, which originated in the work of Freud in the late nineteenth century, represented the first major break with traditional views of mental disorder. Demonic possession was rejected by this approach, as well as the view that such behaviours were the result of illness. According to Freud, we are all in a constant state of conflict and anxiety as a result of the clash between our biological desires (particularly sexual desires) and the restrictions placed upon us by the society in which we live. This conflict can be particularly problematic in early childhood, and can lead to unresolved conflicts being repressed into the unconscious mind. This repression in turn can distort behaviour and lead to mental disorder.

A psychodynamic theory that is currently more influential is **object relations theory** (Klein 1932). This approach views infants as being motivated by the need to relate to others, seen first as part-objects (e.g. the breast) and later as whole objects (e.g. the mother). The infant develops fantasies about these objects based on its own needs, and it is these fantasies, rather than reality, which guide behaviour.

The *behavioural model* is based on the view that all behaviour is learned and on theories about how that learning takes place. It has been summarised best by Eysenck, as follows: 'Freudian theory regards neurotic symptoms as "the visible upshot of unconscious causes". Learning theory does not postulate any such "unconscious" causes, but regards neurotic symptoms as simply learned habits; there is no neurosis underlying the symptom but merely the symptom itself. Get rid of the symptom and you have eliminated the neurosis' (Eysenck 1965, quoted in Tyrer and Steinberg 1987: 49). This model, then, differs from those already discussed in that it does not look for underlying causes, just at observable behaviours. This follows from the fundamental assumption of the behaviourist approach in psychology, which is that observable behaviour, rather than mental processes, either conscious or unconscious, is the main concern of scientific psychology.

The behaviours observed in cases of mental disorder are ones that are regarded as maladaptive. Nevertheless they are acquired in the same way as socially acceptable behaviours. Two major theories of learning have been advanced in order to explain the acquisition of behaviour; these are known as **classical conditioning** and **operant conditioning**. In classical or Pavlovian conditioning, a reflex (or automatic) response comes to be associated with a new stimulus through the conditioning process. An example of this is given in Case study 1.2.

Case study 1.2: Little Albert

In a study by Watson and Rayner (1920), an eleven-month old child called 'Little Albert' was made to fear his pet white rat by the researchers making a loud, frightening noise (striking a steel bar) whenever he was playing with the rat. After seven such episodes, just the sight of the rat was enough to make him cry; in this way, behaviourists argue, phobias could be acquired. Albert's fear spread (or generalised) to other white fluffy objects such as a rabbit, cotton wool and the experimenter's hair.

Operant conditioning (Skinner 1938) is a process whereby the likelihood of a response occurring to a stimulus can be altered depending on whether it has previously been reinforced, for example by a reward being given (which will increase the chance of it occurring again), or punished (which will decrease the chance of it occurring again). For the behaviourists, then, an individual's behaviour patterns will depend on the opportunities provided by the environment to learn through the processes of association, reinforcement and punishment.

The *cognitive model* again presents a contrasting view to those already described, in that it suggests that cognition is the main determinant of behaviour. Thought processes in the conscious mind, including expectations, attitudes, feelings, perceptions and interpretations, can become distorted and lead to disordered behaviour.

One important theoretical contribution to this model is **social learning theory** (Bandura 1969), which proposes that learning occurs through the processes of observation and imitation of the behaviour of others (known as 'models'). Other theorists have focused on the types of faulty thinking shown by those suffering from mental disorder (i.e. the nature of their irrational and maladaptive thoughts). For example, Seligman (1975) refers to a thinking style which he calls 'learned helplessness', and which he believes to be characteristic of depression. People who adopt this style tend to feel that the environment is beyond their control, and that they have no power to influence what happens to them.

The *humanistic/socio-cultural models* (also referred to as the phenomenological or existential models) are not identical by any means, but space precludes separate treatment here. Humanistic theorists aim to look at each person as a unique case and to understand mental problems in terms of that person's view of the world. Rogers (1951), for example, looked at the ways that the individual's self-concept can be distorted by pressure from others (especially family members). The socio-cultural theorists place greater emphasis on the involvement of social forces in the origins of behavioural disorders. For example, the psychiatrist R.D. Laing (1965) felt that mental disorder resulted from anxiety produced by threats to one's individual existence. Many of these writers (e.g. Smail 1991) suggest that the fault lies not in the individual but in the nature of the society in which we live and the way in which we relate to others.

Conclusion

The models outlined have of necessity been described only very briefly to give a better understanding of what follows. It should be emphasised that they need not be seen as mutually exclusive, and the modern approach is to draw on all of them. However, they do lead to different recommendations for treatment, and these will now be described.

> Summarise the main point of each of the models described in the previous section, using just one sentence for each model.
>
> *Progress exercise*

Types of therapeutic approaches

A therapy is a deliberate intervention which aims to treat mental disorder and make it more manageable. A therapy may be an attempt to 'cure' or it may be an attempt to teach the individual how to cope with the problem. What follows is an overview of the range of therapies available. Therapies can be divided broadly into somatic therapies (based on the medical model) and psychotherapies (based on the other models).

Somatic therapy began in the early days of asylums, when 'therapy' was often purely custodial, inmates being kept in chains for the protection of themselves and others. This was changed by Pinel in 1792, whose first move on taking over a Paris asylum called the Bicêtre was to remove all chains and restraints. Even in the early nineteenth century, however, treatments were frequently barbaric. One example is the 'whirling chair', a device into which inmates were strapped and rotated at speed, allegedly until blood ran from their ears.

Currently, somatic therapy has a three-pronged approach, using drugs (known as chemotherapy), electro-convulsive shock therapy (ECT) and/or destruction or functional isolation of brain tissue (psychosurgery). These treatments will be detailed in Chapter 2.

Psychodynamic therapies originate from Freud's system of psychoanalysis. In its original form, the aim was to bring into consciousness those unconscious conflicts which were at the root of the mental disorder, where they could be dealt with by the therapist. To do this required the use of the techniques of free association and dream interpretation, as well as an analysis of the ways in which the client related to the therapist. The latter was thought to reveal, through a process of **transference**, the problems that had occurred in other significant relationships. More recent procedures derived from this include psychoanalytically oriented psychotherapy, and group psychodynamic therapies. There are also psychodynamic therapies based on theorists other than Freud; Klein, for example, has developed her own therapy for adults and play therapy for use with children. These will be described in Chapter 3.

Behavioural therapies will be described in Chapter 4. They fall into two main groups. The first group consists of those based on classical conditioning. These are known as **behaviour therapies**, and they aim to remove maladaptive behaviours by using conditioning procedures. Examples include systematic desensitisation (in which people with irrational fears – of spiders, for example – may be helped to be less fearful) and aversion therapy (in which people who like things that they should not, such as alcohol, will be taught to avoid them).

The second group, **behaviour modification** techniques, is based on operant conditioning procedures. In this case, selective reinforcement is used to encourage desired behaviours and to eliminate undesirable behaviours. The best-known example of this is the token economy system (Allyon and Azrin 1968) where tokens are given as rewards for behaviours that are to be increased, such as being sociable.

Cognitive therapies, which will be described in Chapter 5, can be quite diverse, reflecting as they do a range of different theoretical approaches. They share the common aim of bringing rational thought processes to bear on behaviour and the possibility of change. For example, based on Bandura's (1969) social learning theory, modelling of desired behaviours may be used and imitation encouraged. Role play can also be used (e.g. in **personal construct therapy**) to challenge the individual's self-concept. Following Beck's (1967) approach, irrational beliefs can be challenged by discussion or by setting tasks that put them to the test.

Humanistic therapies, such as Rogers' person-centered therapy (1980), aim to encourage personal growth and development by providing, in the therapeutic relationship, an environment in which this is possible. Unlike many of the approaches mentioned earlier, the individual is encouraged to take control of their situation and to make decisions without the intervention of the therapist. Other approaches developed from this include encounter groups and family therapy, where the way that individuals communicate with and relate to one another is used as a basis for treating their behaviour disorders. These therapies will be described in Chapter 6. It should be noted that many psychologists who subscribe to the socio-cultural model feel that intervention on a larger, societal scale will be required to fully solve the problems faced by many people, but such interventions are beyond the scope of this book.

Chapter summary

In this chapter we have outlined the different criteria for defining abnormal behaviour, with emphasis on the mental illness criterion. The classification system DSM IV has been described and evaluated briefly. The different models which attempt to understand such behaviour – medical, psychodynamic, behavioural, cognitive and humanistic/socio-cultural – have been explained. The implications of each of these models for treatment, and the range of therapies available within each group have also been described. In Chapters 2 to 6 the somatic, behavioural, cognitive and humanistic/socio-cultural therapies will be considered individually.

For each model of mental disorder, draw up a summary table to show the model's view of the origins of mental disorder, the theoretical basis (or bases), and an example of a therapeutic approach derived from the model.

Review exercise

Further reading

Gross, R. and McIlveen (1996) *Abnormal Psychology*, London: Hodder & Stoughton. (An interesting and reasonably-priced text that is up-to-date and gives concise but thorough coverage of the area as a whole.)

Davison, G. and Neale, J. (1994) *Abnormal Psychology* (6th edition), NY: Wiley. (A more expensive text, but well-presented and well-detailed.)

Somatic therapies

General principles

Somatic therapies are derived from the medical model, which views mental disorder as an illness. Treatment therefore revolves around a range of bodily (or 'somatic') approaches. Those which will be discussed here are drugs, electro-convulsive shock therapy (ECT) and psychosurgery.

Drug therapy

Drug therapy is also known as chemotherapy. Drugs were first used to treat mental disorder in the nineteenth century. Since the 1950s their use has become widespread, and they account for a large proportion of NHS prescriptions. In 1979, for example, 30.7 million prescriptions for Benzodiazepines (one type of minor tranquilliser) were dispensed (Taylor 1987).

The main types of drug used are:

- major tranquillisers (also known as antipsychotic or neuroleptic drugs)
- minor tranquillisers (anti-anxiety or anxiolytic drugs)
- antidepressants
- anti-manic drugs
- stimulants

Although the proprietary names for these change regularly, Table 2.1 gives a list of those currently in use.

Table 2.1 Major drugs used to treat mental disorder

Major tran-quillisers	Minor tran-quillisers	Antidepres-sants	Anti-manics	Stimulants
Phenothia-zines e.g. chlorpromazine *Thorazine*, *Largactil*)	Propanediol e.g. meproba-mate *Miltown*)	Monoamine Oxidase Inhibitors e.g. phenelzine *Nardil*	Lithium e.g. lithium carbonate *Lithane*, lithium citrate *Litarex*	Ampheta-mines e.g. dexadrine, methedrine, amphetamine sulphate *Ritalin*
Butyro-phenones e.g. halperidol *Haldol*, droperidol *Droleptan*	Benzodiazep-ines e.g. chlor-diazepoxide *Librium*, diazepam *Valium*, temazepam *Euhypnos*, nitrazepam *Mogadon*, lorazepam *Ativan*, alpra-zolam *Xanax*	Tricyclics e.g. imipramine *Tofranil*		
Dibezazepines e.g. clozapine *Clozaril*		Selective Serotonin Reuptake Inhibitors e.g. fluoxetine *Prozac*, sertra-line *Lustral*, clomipramine *Anafranil*		

Note: words in italics are trade-names

These drugs typically operate by affecting transmission in the nervous system. A detailed description of how this happens is beyond the scope of this book, but a very brief account follows (for a fuller account see the book entitled *The Physiological Basis of Behaviour* in this series). Although neural transmission is mainly electrical in nature (a nerve impulse being an electrical charge that travels along a nerve), transmission at the junction between nerves (known as the synaptic cleft) is brought about by chemical means. Chemicals known as **neurotransmitters** are produced by nerve cells to do this. There are many different types of neurotransmitter, the main ones being **dopamine**, **serotonin**, acetylcholine, **noradrenaline** (also known as norepinephrine) and gamma-amino butyric acid (**GABA**). Psychoactive drugs operate in many different ways, but basically the outcome is to increase or decrease the levels of available neurotransmitter. Depending on which neurotransmitter they affect, and whether they enhance or diminish its effectiveness, they can have calming or energising effects on different kinds of behaviour. The different methods of action of different drugs also means that they have different side-effects.

We can now consider each group of drugs in turn, in terms of what they are used for, how they work and what the problems and side effects might be.

Major tranquillisers (antipsychotic drugs)

As the name implies, these are used to treat severe disorders such as **schizophrenia**. They act to reduce the level of dopamine in the brain by blocking certain types of receptors (called D2 and D4 receptors) for dopamine in the nervous system. Their beneficial effects include a general calming effect, and the reduction of psychotic symptoms such as hallucinations, confusion, and movement disorders. However, they have little effect on such negative symptoms as withdrawal and listlessness, and have some significant side effects such as blurred vision, dry mouth, poor concentration, and low blood pressure. Some types of major tranquillisers are associated with an increased tendency to burn in the sun, impotence in males, and irreversible abnormalities in movement such as **tardive dyskinesia** (involuntary tics and spasms, and uncontrollable writhing of the tongue). Tardive dyskinesia occurs in around 30 per cent of patients and is more likely to be seen with prolonged use of the drug (Gaultieri 1991), in older patients and in those on higher doses (Hughes and Pierattini 1992). Other types of major tranquilliser, such as clozapine, are more effective for some patients and are not associated with movement disorders. However, they can lead to a fatal inhibition of white blood cell production, called agranulocytosis, in a small percentage of patients. This leads to increased susceptibility to infectious diseases. The presence of such problems means that other drugs may be needed to control the side effects, and that regular blood tests will be necessary to monitor white blood cell counts. A recent version of this type of 'atypical antipsychotic', called olanzapine, is thought not to affect the white blood cell count in this way.

Although such drugs do not appear to help all sufferers, and long-term use may not be possible, it has been found that they can be more effective than other therapies (including the use of **placebos**, or 'dummy drugs') for these disorders, and they may help to prevent relapse (Hogarty *et al.* 1974). Phenothiazines, for example, have been found to be associated with improvement in 60 to 70 per cent of patients (Bernstein *et al.* 1994).

Minor tranquillisers

Also known as **anxiolytic** drugs, these are used to reduce anxiety and muscle tension, and help to calm people who are suffering from a wide range of neuroses, from phobias to generalised anxiety disorder. Alprazolam, for example, has been found to be helpful in the treatment of panic disorder and agoraphobia (Klosko *et al.* 1990). They may also be useful with stress-related disorders and with reactive depression, as well as helping people who are undergoing withdrawal from alcohol and drug addiction.

These drugs operate by depressing activity in the Central Nervous System, which in turn reduces activity in the Sympathetic Nervous System. This is responsible for the physiological changes (such as increase in heart rate) which are associated with emotional responses. The sensitivity of receptors to GABA is also increased; because GABA is an inhibitory transmitter, blocking responses, this leads to the inhibition of behaviour.

The side effects of these drugs can again be considerable, especially with long-term use. As well as lethargy, **dependency** on the drug develops (i.e. there is a need to keep on taking it), along with increased **tolerance** (needing to take more of the drug to achieve the desired effect) and **withdrawal** symptoms such as tremors, convulsions and increased anxiety when the drug is no longer used. The drugs are also toxic, so an overdose can lead to death, especially if combined with alcohol. However, a more recent drug in this group, buspirone, is slower acting but does not promote dependence, interact with alcohol or cause cognitive or motor impairment (Lickey and Gordon 1991). It affects serotonin receptors rather than GABA receptors. Despite the apparent lack of side effects, 10 per cent of patients still stop using it (Okocha 1998).

Although use of these drugs is now falling (King *et al.* 1990), many writers feel that they have been misused as a method of social control (Gabe 1996), particularly in the treatment of women. When pressure to comply with traditional gender roles produces symptoms of mental disorder, it could be argued that the use of medication to alleviate symptoms condones such social pressures (Cooperstock and Lennard 1979).

Antidepressants

These are used to elevate the mood of depressive patients, and to reduce panic in anxious patients. They may therefore be given for anxiety, agoraphobia, obsessive-compulsive disorder, panic attacks, eating disorders and Seasonal Affective Disorder as well as for simple depression. Clomipramine, for example, has been used to treat obsessive-compulsive disorder (Leonard *et al.* 1989). They can be divided into three major groups according to the way in which they achieve their effects; the outcome in all cases is enhancement of the action of one or more neurotransmitters.

The **monoamine oxidase inhibitors** (MAOIs) block the action of the enzyme monoamine oxidase, which normally breaks down the neurotransmitters noradrenaline and serotonin. Thus MAOIs increase the levels of these neurotransmitters in the nervous system. The **tricyclics** (TCAs) prevent the same neurotransmitters from being re-absorbed after use, in effect also increasing the available levels. The **selective serotonin re-uptake inhibitors** (SSRIs) increase the level of available serotonin by preventing its re-uptake.

One drawback with the use of antidepressants is that it may be several weeks before any beneficial effects are seen (Marks and O'Sullivan 1988). This is a little puzzling, since the effects of such drugs on neurotransmitter levels are almost instantaneous. Side effects are also found; these vary according to the type of antidepressant used. The MAOIs and TCAs are 'dirty' compounds, which affect a number of bodily systems. The MAOIs are the least used, and most of them require dietary restrictions so that the patient avoids foods such as cheese, chocolate, yeast, bananas, yoghurt, alcohol and chicken livers, all of which contain the protein tyramine. When combined with tyramine, MAOIs can produce hypertension, which can in turn result in a brain haemorrhage. They also have dangerous interactions with other drugs such as cold remedies. Side effects include urinary retention, damage to the liver and cardiovascular system, cardiac arrhythmias, dry mouth and blurred vision. There is a new class of MAOI drugs, however, which do not have these effects (Julien 1992). These are known as RIMAs, or reversible inhibitors of monoamine oxidase (e.g. moclobemide).

Tricyclics have side effects such as dizziness, blurred vision, sweating, weight gain, constipation, poor concentration, impaired short-term memory (Richardson *et al.* 1994), sleepiness and dry mouth. In older people particularly, they can impair driving to a greater extent than being over the limit for alcohol (Edwards 1995). The newer SSRIs, such as Prozac, have fewer side effects, although they can still cause nausea, stomach upsets, insomnia, dizziness, headaches, nervousness and impaired sexual functioning (known as 'serotinergic syndrome'). They are safer in overdose and less likely to impair driving than the other antidepressants, but at the same time they are very expensive and have recently been suspected of being linked with increased levels of aggression and suicidal thoughts (Steiner 1991). Other drugs such as anti-histamines, cold preparations, travel sickness pills and some pain killers cannot be taken at the same time as these SSRIs, or they will produce an adverse reaction.

General evaluation

Antidepressant drugs are an effective way to treat depression and anxiety in the short term, significantly helping 60 to 80 per cent of people according to some reports (Bernstein *et al.* 1994). However, they are not equally effective in all cases and may not be better than psychotherapy in the long term (NIMH 1987). A recent and controversial study by Kirsch and Sapirstein (1998) analysed the results from nineteen studies, covering 2,318 patients who had been treated with antidepressants. They found that antidepressants were only 25 per cent more effective than placebos, and no more effective than other kinds of drugs, such as tranquillisers.

In addition, many patients do not like to take drugs. A **meta-analysis** of studies by Anderson and Tomenson (1995) found drop-out rates to be 30 per cent for patients taking TCAs and 27 per cent for SSRIs. The drop-out rates due to side effects alone were 20 per cent for TCAs and 15 per cent for SSRIs.

Antimanic drugs

These drugs are used to treat manic-depression (also known as **bipolar affective disorder**). The main drug used is lithium, which may operate in two ways. First, it may decrease the levels of the neurotransmitters noradrenaline and serotonin by stimulating their re-uptake or preventing their release. Second, it may stabilise nerve cell membranes and hence reduce transmission in the nervous system. This has the effect of normalising manic patients rapidly and stabilising mood over the long term.

Although most patients respond within six to eight days, the drugs can take up to a year to be effective in stabilising mood. They are helpful for up to 80 per cent of sufferers, leading to a significant reduction in hospital admissions and in duration of stay. Antimanic drugs are also useful as a preventative measure; taken in this way, they can forestall future mood swings (Prien *et al.* 1984). On the other hand, discontinuing use can increase the risk of future manic-depressive episodes (Suppes *et al.* 1991). The side effects include tremors, dry mouth, nausea, stomach pains, weight gain, kidney poisoning and memory impairment. Blood concentration needs to be checked at four to eight week intervals because lithium is a toxin, and the effective dose is one that is close to toxic levels. (See Case study 2.1.)

Case study 2.1: bipolar disorder

Suzanne was a university student who was referred for treatment after a suicide attempt. She had a history of manic episodes which had led her to do things like staying up all night to write a book, and telephoning her parents in the middle of the night. On the basis of her mood swings and general level of agitation and distractability she was diagnosed as suffering from bipolar disorder. Lithium was prescribed to stabilise her mood, but she found it difficult to persevere with the treatment. This was because the side effects were unpleasant, and she became bored without the excitement generated by her manic episodes. Psychotherapy was used to teach her how to identify symptoms that could signal the onset of a new episode, and she was able to take lower maintenance doses to reduce the side effects (Clipson and Steer 1998).

Stimulants

These drugs increase alertness and feelings of confidence, and elevate mood in most people. Stimulants were originally used to treat lethargic, depressed patients. Their main use is with hyperactive children who, paradoxical though it may seem, can show improved concentration after taking stimulants. The drugs operate to block the re-uptake of noradrenaline and dopamine, as well as stimulating the receptors for these neurotransmitters. Their main side effect is dependence – tolerance develops – and there may be interference with sleep, appetite and learning. For this reason they are best used in the short term only, in combination with behaviour therapy (Gittleman-Klein *et al.* 1976). An example is given in Case study 2.2.

Case study 2.2: a hyperactive child

Richard was referred for treatment because of his disruptive classroom behaviour and inability to concentrate. Psychological assessment revealed that he was suffering from

Attention Deficit Hyperactivity Disorder (ADHD). This is characterised by achievement deficits despite at least average intelligence, and difficulties with sequencing and organising behaviour, as well as self-regulation. He was given the drug Ritalin, a stimulant related to amphetamine, which is effective in 70 to 90 per cent of such cases. Psychotherapy was also used to improve his social skills, ability to plan and to exert self control. He eventually graduated from school, and went on to college; he no longer needs to take the medication (Clipson and Steer 1998).

Evaluation of drug therapy

In general, drugs have been extremely effective in reducing the numbers of hospital in-patients who are being treated for mental disorder (but note that such reductions in numbers also reflect changing policies towards hospitalisation). Drugs provide effective long-term control for mood disorders and psychotic illnesses, and may help to prevent suicide in depressive patients and to reduce anxiety in neurotic patients.

The side effects observed represent the main drawback, and raise important ethical issues. Unless treatment is regarded as an emergency, it cannot be given without the patient's consent (except where the patient may be deemed to be incapable of giving consent). This consent should be given on the basis of full information about the potential benefits and drawbacks of the drug(s) concerned, in which case it fulfils the ethical criterion of **informed consent**. Apart from the side effects, the main criticism of drug treatments is that although they are effective in reducing the symptoms of mental disorder, they do not constitute a cure and have therefore been seen by some writers as merely a chemical straitjacket.

Progress exercise

Before reading on, see if you can remember:

1 The five main types of psychoactive drug
2 One named example of each
3 Which disorder each type is used to treat
4 One cost and one benefit of each type

Look back over the section to check your answers.

Electro-convulsive shock therapy (ECT)

Attempts to alleviate psychoses by inducing comas or epileptic-type seizures date back to Sakel in 1938, who used insulin injections to produce comas. In the same decade, von Meduna observed (incorrectly!) that schizophrenia and epilepsy did not occur together in the same patient, and thought that inducing an epileptic fit would therefore eliminate schizophrenia. He used various drugs to induce convulsions, but it was Cerletti and Bini in 1938 who initiated the use of an electric shock across the temples to do this.

The procedure is now used to treat severe depression, not schizophrenia. When first introduced, it caused such severe muscle spasms that broken bones could result, and the treatment was also associated with cell death in the cerebral cortex of the brain. Side effects reported included memory loss, speech disorders and even cardiac arrest (Lickey and Gordon 1991). Modern procedures involve reduced shock levels and muscle relaxants, as well as the administration of a general anaesthetic so that patients find the experience less frightening. As this is not classed as an emergency treatment, the patient's informed consent must also be obtained (unless the patient is considered incapable of giving this, in which case a second medical opinion must be sought). Electrical current is applied via electrodes positioned on the head, either bilaterally (one on either side of the head) or unilaterally (both on the same side of the head – usually the non-dominant cerebral hemisphere, which is on the right side for right-handed people). Current of 110mv (200ma) is passed for between half a second to five seconds, causing only slight facial twitches to appear. Consciousness is regained after about five to twenty minutes. Usually a series of four to six such treatments will be given over a period of several weeks.

Evaluation of ECT

The treatment has been shown to be effective for depression in 60 to 70 per cent of patients (Sackheim 1988). With suicidal patients it has the advantage that it is extremely rapid, and these days it is regarded as being one of the safest medical treatments available (Smith 1977; cited by Gross 1992). Consequently it is the preferred treatment for severe depression during pregnancy. However, Breggin (1979) demonstrated that brain damage can occur following its administration to animals. Another criticism is based on a survey of 308 patients, which showed that two-thirds of them did not regard the treatment as helpful, and half of those also felt that it had in fact been damaging (UKAN 1995). Where it is useful, the effects may only be short-term (Sackheim *et al.* 1993).

One drawback with ECT is that it can cause memory disruption; in particular, knowledge of events occurring immediately prior to treatment may be disrupted for several weeks afterwards. This is felt to be less of a problem now that the electrical current administered is reduced and shocks are more often unilateral rather than bilateral.

The other main objection is the ethical point that the mechanism by which ECT works is still not known, which has led some writers to describe it as being as scientific as kicking the television to make it work (Heather 1976). Benton (1981) has suggested three possibilities:

1   Because it is such an unpleasant process, it may simply be acting as a punishment. However, this is unlikely to be the case, as smaller shocks which do not produce convulsions are equally unpleasant but are ineffective as treatments.
2   The memory loss which occurs permits cognitive restructuring and change in habitual thought processes. This too is unlikely because unilateral shocks produce minimal memory loss but are still effective treatments.
3   Biochemical changes (e.g. in the levels of glucose, neurotransmitters and protein synthesis) may be stimulated, or there may be changes in the permeability of cell membranes. This seems to be the most likely possibility at present, but there is no research evidence to support the idea.

23

Progress exercise

Draw up a table to show the advantages and disadvantages of ECT.

Psychosurgery

Psychosurgery is the use of brain surgery to destroy a small area or to isolate an area by cutting its connections with the rest of the brain. If the area concerned is malfunctioning, this procedure should alleviate the mental disorder that the area is producing. There are several different operations that have been devised to do this.

The **prefrontal lobotomy** (or leucotomy) was introduced by Moniz in 1935 as a result of his finding that aggression in chimpanzees could be reduced by removing part of the frontal lobes. His technique was to drill into the skull at the side and sever the connections inside with a blunt instrument. Between 1935 and 1949 one hundred such operations were carried out. Although Moniz claimed a 70 per cent success rate and in 1949 was awarded the Nobel prize, the fact that he was shot by one of his own patients suggests that the technique was not entirely successful!

Following this, Freeman and Watts devised a **transorbital lobotomy** which involved inserting a sharp instrument into the brain through the socket (or 'orbit') of the eye. This became popular in America, where 25–40,000 operations have been carried out since the late 1930s, mostly to alleviate schizophrenia and depression.

Since the 1950s and the introduction of drug treatment, these approaches have become much less popular, often being used only as a last resort. Snaith (1994) has estimated that only about twenty operations per year are carried out in the UK at present, although other estimates give figures up to fifty. The main uses are to treat severe anxiety and depression, or obsessive-compulsive disorder. Refined surgical techniques mean that very precise damage can now be caused to clearly-defined areas. Lobotomies now involve drilling two small holes in the forehead through which radioactive rods can be inserted; electrical probes or lasers can also be used to burn out tissue in selected areas. For example, a bilateral stereotactic subcaudate tracto-tomy cuts the pathway between the limbic system and the hypothalamus (two small structures deep inside the brain, see Figure 2.1) and is used to treat depression. Obsessive-compulsive disorder is treated by a **cingulotomy**, which cuts the connections between the prefrontal cortex and the limbic system (Hay *et al.* 1993). Aggressive and violent patients can be treated with a *limbic leucotomy*.

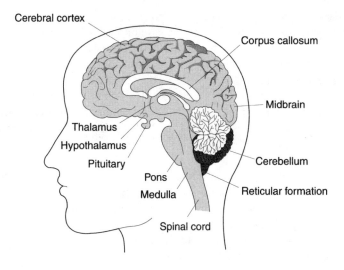

Figure 2.1   **A front-to-back cross-section of the brain, showing its major structures. (Note that the limbic system and basal ganglia surround the areas of the hypothalamus and the thalamus, but are difficult to depict in a two-dimensional illus-tration.)**

Source: McIlveen, R. and Gross, R. (1996) *Biopsychology*, London: Hodder and Stoughton, p. 18.

Evaluation of psychosurgery

Modern psychosurgery techniques appear to cause less intellectual and emotional impairment than some of the earlier techniques, which had serious side effects such as major personality change and even death. For example, Baer *et al.* (1995) reported a long-term follow-up study of eighteen people who had cingulotomies for obsessive-compulsive disorder because they had not responded to psychotherapy. They showed improved functioning, were less depressed and anxious and had few negative side effects. However, psychosurgery is not always successful, nor is it always clear why it works when it does, or exactly what the effects will be in any one case. Since the operations are irreversible, side effects are also permanent. These have included reduced creativity, epileptic seizures, emotional blunting, impaired learning ability, overeating, memory loss, paralysis and indifference. Perhaps for this reason, psychosurgery is generally reserved for only the most intractable cases, meaning those which have proved resistant to drugs and psychotherapy. It also requires the authority of an independent doctor as well as the informed consent of the patient. An example of a recent development in psychosurgery which may prove to be less problematic is outlined in Case study 2.3.

Case study 2.3: the use of brain surgery to treat stuttering (*Fox* et al. *1997*)

Stuttering is often considered to be a psychological disorder and has been treated with psychotherapy. Fox and his colleagues compared the brain scans of stutterers and non-stutterers and discovered that different areas of the brain are active when they try to speak. Stutterers show activity in an area of the right hemisphere responsible for planning movement, whilst non-stutterers show activity in the corresponding area of the left hemisphere responsible for language skills. **Transcranial magnetic stimulation** (TMS) is being used to create a temporary lesion in the area identified in stutterers to see if their condition improves. TMS could then be re-applied when the effects wear off, rather than using surgery to create a permanent lesion.

Other somatic approaches

It is appropriate here to mention some of modern approaches that are trying to tackle the problem of mental disorder in different ways, but can still be linked with the medical approach. One is the use of **phototherapy** to treat **Seasonal Affective Disorder**, a depressive condition that affects sufferers in the winter months (although there is a summer form as well). This disorder has been linked with hormonal disruption due to the reduced hours of daylight in winter, and treatment has therefore taken the form of exposure to bright light (six times the intensity of normal indoor lighting) for two hours daily (Wehr and Rosenthal 1989). Even more recently, dawn simulators have been tested, which aim to increase the morning light levels in the bedroom gradually, just as they do naturally in summer.

Another possibility is based on research that links nutrition and behaviour. Hyperactive children, for example, have been shown to be allergic to certain foods, food additives or environmental toxins, and adult psychiatric patients have also been shown to be intolerant to substances such as caffeine and chocolate. Dietary interventions, such as preventing hyperactive children from consuming drinks containing the additive tartrazine, have been found to be beneficial in some cases. The Feingold diet (1975), for example, involves the avoidance of flavourings, colourings and preservatives, both artificial and natural. However, Conners (1980) found that dietary intervention yielded only a 5 per cent success rate. It has been suggested that the beneficial effects may be the result of increased feelings of control that result from adhering to a diet, rather than the diet itself.

Applicability and evaluation

Since individual approaches have been considered at the end of each section, only general points will be made here.

Although effective in many cases of mental disorder (not all, by any means), somatic therapy has many drawbacks. In particular, it overlooks the important point that factors other than medical conditions are involved in many mental disorders, if not all, and that the medical basis of most disorders remains obscure. Szasz (1962) would argue on this basis that medical treatment is inappropriate for problems which are essentially social in their origins. If this is the case, then perhaps the best use for many of the somatic therapies may be to relieve some of the major symptoms of disorder so that psychotherapy can be used to bring about more lasting change. Case studies 2.1 and 2.2 illustrate this point well.

Chapter summary

In this chapter we have seen that somatic therapy relies on the use of drugs, ECT and psychosurgery. The drugs used may be major tranquillisers (for psychosis), minor tranquillisers (for anxiety disorders), antidepressants (for depression and anxiety), antimanic drugs (for bipolar disorder) or stimulants (for hyperactivity). ECT, the administration of electric shocks to the brain, is used for the treatment of severe depression. Psychosurgery, the removal or isolation of part of the brain, has been used to treat obsessive-compulsive disorder and extreme depression. All of these treatments can be effective, but have undesirable side effects which must be taken into account. This is particularly the case when the effects are permanent. Some of the somatic treatments can also be criticised because they give only temporary relief rather than providing a permanent cure. Ethical issues must also be considered, and the informed consent of the patient obtained prior to treatment.

Sample essay question

(a) Describe treatments which are based on the somatic approach to mental illness. (12 marks)
(b) Discuss the difficulties involved in evaluating the effectiveness of these treatments. (12 marks)[1] [AEB, June 1995]

. . . .

1 The individual marks for these parted questions have been adjusted to correspond with the current mark scheme.

Review exercise

Use the following words to fill in the blanks in the passage below. Use each word once only:

cure; tranquillisers; informed; side effects; ECT; irreversible; unknown; depression; anti manic.

Somatic therapy relies on the use of drugs, ——, and psychosurgery to treat mental disorder. There are five groups of drugs: major ——; minor tranquillisers, stimulants and —— drugs. They are generally effective in the short-term, but do not represent a —— and have serious ——. ECT is used to treat ——, where it can be effective in some severe cases, but its mode of action is ——. Psychosurgery is an unpredictable technique which is unpopular because it is also——. To comply with ethical requirements, the patient's —— consent must be obtained before treatment takes place.

(The answers are as follows: ECT; tranquillisers; antimanic; cure; side effects; depression; unknown; irreversible; informed.)

Further reading

Gabe, J. (1996) 'The history of tranquilliser use', in T. Heller *et al.* (eds) *Mental Health Matters: A Reader*, London: Macmillan. (An excellent outline and critique of this area.)

Silber, K. (1999) *The Physiological Basis Of Behaviour*, London: Routledge. (Gives a clear summary of the structure and functioning of the nervous system, and the effects of drugs, which is useful background for understanding somatic therapies.)

3

Psychodynamic therapies

General principles

All psychodynamic therapies derive ultimately from the work of Freud and his immediate followers, Jung and Adler. Freud's studies with Charcot in 1885 and Breuer in 1895, investigating treatments for hysteria and other neuroses, led to the development of psychoanalysis in 1897. The new treatment caught on rapidly and had an international reputation by 1910. Its spread in Europe was restricted during the Second World War by Nazi disapproval (Freud being Jewish), and it became more established in the US and Britain, where many analysts had taken refuge during the war.

Freudian theory divides personality into three parts: the *id* (unconscious, instinctive); the *superego* (moral aspect); and the *ego* (an intermediary which deals with reality and tries to appease both the id and the superego). According to this approach, anxiety results from the inability of the ego to manage conflicts arising from instinctual urges (the id) and the demands of society for moral constraints on behaviour (the superego). This is the main cause of mental disorder. Different symptoms will result from the different defence mechanisms used to reduce anxiety. All symptoms have causes, but the causes will not be available to the conscious mind since they are buried deep in the unconscious.

Psychoanalysis aims to effect a cure by uncovering these unconscious conflicts (called 'making the unconscious conscious') in the course of analysis and by helping the patient to deal with them rationally. This should release the patient from neurotic disorders and lead to a fundamental personality change. Psychoanalysts believe that simply treating the symptom (a policy pursued by some therapies dealt with in other chapters) will not cure the root of the problem. It may well result in **symptom substitution**, whereby a replacement disorder develops. Thus psychoanalysis typically involves two stages: first, removing repressions, so that the patient becomes consciously aware of the conflict and its origins, and thus gains insight; second, helping the ego to deal with the conflict in more appropriate ways.

Freudian psychoanalysis

Psychoanalysis itself employs four main techniques to uncover unconscious conflicts:

- free association
- transference
- use of leakages of information through parapraxes, body language and physiological cues
- dream interpretation

These are followed by interpretative comment from the therapist and time spent working through the conflict. The whole process takes place in a therapeutic environment which is carefully designed to encourage feelings of safety and confidentiality. A couch may be used to encourage the patient to relax, and the therapist will then sit unobtrusively behind the patient.

Although Freud originally started by using hypnosis to access the patient's unconscious, he found that it was unreliable in the sense that not all patients were hypnotisable, nor were they able to accept that reports given under hypnosis were accurate. Even worse, they some-times simply went to sleep! Therefore he substituted the technique of **free association**, which requires the patient to say whatever comes to mind, however trivial it seems, without censorship. The idea behind this was that when censorship is suspended there is more chance of unconscious material slipping past into consciousness.

Another way to access the unconscious is to examine **parapraxes** or Freudian slips. According to the principle of psychic determinism, all of our behaviour has a cause, including accidents and slips of the tongue. For example, to refer to the 'copulation explosion' instead of the 'population explosion' could be regarded as a significant 'prod' from the id. Other ways in which unconscious material could slip out, which modern analysts are also alert to, include physiological reactions such as blushing and non-verbal cues such as tone of voice and posture.

Dream interpretation is one of the techniques that Freud is most famous for. He considered that dreams, because they occur during sleep when defences are lowered, are symbolic expressions of unconscious material; they therefore represent the 'royal road to the unconscious'. The patient's report of the dream was termed the 'manifest content'. This is produced from unconscious material (or 'latent content') by unconscious distorting processes known collectively as '**dreamwork**'. These act to substitute disturbing images (e.g. a penis) with less disturbing symbols (e.g. a snake). Symbols can also represent abstract ideas, such as the use of a crown to represent power. In order to interpret a dream, the analyst may examine it in conjunction with the patient's free associations to their own dream content, reports about the previous day's happenings (which are often worked into the dream), and in conjunction with other dreams that may form part of a series. An example of a dream and its interpretation is given in Case study 3.1.

Case study 3.1: Freud's interpretation of a woman's dream

The woman concerned had recently become engaged but the marriage had had to be postponed. The dream was of arranging flowers for a birthday celebration. An expensive bunch of violets, lilies and pink carnations were being arranged so that the untidy parts were covered up with green paper.

The interpretation was that the flowers represented the woman's genitals, and her wish to consummate her marriage. The birthday referred to was the birth of a baby. The flowers were expensive, representing the value placed on virginity. Lilies represent purity, violets represent violation, and carnations pink flesh-colour. Covering up the untidy parts refers to the woman being aware of her physical deficiencies.

Transference is a process whereby the patient transfers feelings and fantasies about significant others onto the therapist. The relationship with the therapist then becomes a way of re-enacting these previous relationships, and can reveal a great deal about the nature of unconscious conflicts. There is an attachment to the therapist and often jealousy as well, leading to hostility and aggression.

Countertransference can also occur, where the therapist finds it difficult to remain neutral because of his own unresolved emotional difficulties. For example, the patient may be seen as a daughter figure. During training, therapists undergo analysis themselves to make them more aware of this possibility. Modern analysts tend to see it not so much as a failing but as an unavoidable occurrence that can provide them with even greater insight into the patient's problems.

Use of techniques

All of the techniques outlined above aim to increase levels of conscious awareness and to provide material for therapists to use for the purposes of interpretation. Thus the therapist will respond at the appropriate moment with interpretative comments which aim to clarify the repressed feelings and conflicts underlying behaviour. Such interpretations may both depend on and lead to **resistances** by the patient regarding what is happening. An interpretation is a hypothesis about how a resistance operates, why it is being used and what it is trying to keep out of consciousness. Examples of interpretations are given in Case study 3.2.

Case study 3.2: the Wolf Man – a Freudian case study (1918)

This patient, the twenty-three year old son of a wealthy Russian, was referred for treatment because he was unable to deal with any aspect of everyday life, including dressing himself. At the age of four his behaviour had become disruptive and he had developed a phobia of wolves. He later identified with Christ and developed many obsessive thoughts and compulsive rituals. He had made sexual advances to his sister, and had had sexual encounters with female servants, leading to infection with gonorrhoea.

In the course of therapy, the patient recalled that at the age of four he had been threatened with castration by a nanny and wished to obtain revenge on her. This showed itself in his dreams of tearing the wings off wasps. The wolf phobia was explained as an expression of conflict resulting from emotional feelings for his father. The patient feared that his father would castrate him if he were aware of these feelings, so he used the wolf as a father substitute. By seeing the wolf as the source of his fear, he was able to locate danger and anxiety outside himself instead of admitting to internal danger or castration anxiety. The change to obsessive behaviour was accounted for by the formation of the superego (or conscience) at this time, which led the patient to experience moral anxiety (due to the unacceptable nature of his impulses) instead of castration anxiety. This internalised the problem again, and it was repressed into the unconscious by the ego, leading to an obsessional neurosis.

The use of interpretations will hopefully lead to the patient achieving **insight** into the reasons for behaviour and the origins of unconscious conflicts. This self-knowledge can then be used as the basis for **working through** the implications of the conflict and finding ways of dealing with it more effectively than before. The distorted behaviours and defence mechanisms used should then become unnecessary, and a lasting change in personality is possible. Termination of analysis is then the final task; often a traumatic process in itself, it must be done with care and when the time is right for the patient to become independent again.

Evaluation of psychoanalysis

Psychoanalysis is best suited to the treatment of **neuroses**. Freud himself regarded it as unsuitable for psychotic patients and as requiring a reasonable level of education, an assessment confirmed by Luborsky and Spence (1978). Later writers such as Boker (1992) have argued that these criteria are not essential. Psychoanalysis is often described as most suitable for patients who display the **YAVIS syndrome**, that is to say they are young, attractive, verbal, intelligent and successful.

On the negative side, psychoanalysis is a lengthy process, involving five one-hour sessions per week for a minimum of two years. At times during this process the patient will be extremely vulnerable psychologically. It can also be a costly process, partly because it is so lengthy and partly because it is not generally available on the National Health Service. Another problem is that both psychoanalysis and the Freudian theory derived from it are widely regarded as lacking in scientific support (e.g. Grunbaum 1984). Many of the ideas cannot be subjected to rigorous testing as it is not possible to derive explicit predictions about behaviour from them. After the event, on the other hand, it is possible to explain virtually any outcome in psychodynamic terms.

The credibility of Freud's case studies has also been questioned (Masson 1988) because in many cases the facts appear to have been distorted. Anna O., for example, one of Freud's best known cases, was in fact far from cured by her analysis and suffered many relapses. In other cases, Freud would appear to have shown considerable bias in his dealings with patients. For example, his claims that patients' reports of sexual abuse by relatives were purely fantasies have been questioned. Both therapy and reporting can therefore be regarded as potentially manipulative. An example of this is given in Case study 3.3.

Case study 3.3: the case of Dora (Freud 1905)

Dora (real name Ida Bauer) was referred to Freud by her father in 1900, at the age of eighteen. Her problems were depression, a nervous cough, loss of voice, and inability to relate to her family and their friends. She had recently fainted while arguing with her father, and had written a suicide note. Her father was having an affair with Frau K., a family friend, and Herr K., her husband, had made sexual advances to Dora when she was just fourteen, attempting to kiss her when they were alone together. He subsequently denied this and persuaded Dora's father that she had imagined it.

Freud's analysis was that Dora was in love with her father and with Herr K. Hence she was jealous of Frau K and had fantasised the sexual abuse. When Dora rejected this, Freud put it down to resistance. When she terminated analysis after just three months, he attributed it to her desire for revenge on men. The case was written up as if she had been cured, and it included his first description of the transference process and its effects on treatment. Subsequent investigations (Masson 1988) indicate that although Dora was often described as being 'a disagreeable creature' her main problem may have been that no-one believed what she said. Freud's failure to accept her version of events simply compounded the problem. As Marcus (1985) has written 'Dora refused to be a character in the story that Freud was composing for her'.

The effectiveness of psychoanalysis will be considered more fully in the general discussion about evaluation of therapies in Chapter 8, but it should be pointed out here that many critics such as Eysenck (1965) have claimed that it is no more effective than a placebo (or 'dummy') treatment. However, critics of Eysenck, such as Bergin (1971), have argued that a re-analysis of the data used by Eysenck shows that improvement was evident in 83 per cent of cases, compared with 30 per cent of those given placebo treatment. Assessment of outcome is further complicated by the fact that in many cases, due to the long duration of therapy, it is possible that symptoms may disappear of their own accord (known as **spontaneous remission**) rather than as a result of the therapy itself.

Progress exercise

See if you can remember what the following analytic techniques involve: free association; parapraxes; transference; counter-transference; interpretation; resistance; insight; working through. Look back over the previous section to check your ideas.

Modern psychodynamic approaches

As well as the classical psychoanalytic approach just described, there are four modern developments that can be mentioned here: Kleinian psychodynamic therapy; play therapy; psychoanalytically oriented psychotherapies; and psychodynamic group therapies.

Kleinian psychodynamic therapy

One of the most popular psychodynamic approaches in Britain today is based on **object relations theory** as described by Klein (1882–1960). Unconscious processes and early childhood experiences are emphasised in this approach, but the main focus is on the nature of early relationships with significant others. Whether such relationships are satisfying or frustrating is an important determinant of the way in which other people are viewed in later life. This can affect the individual's ability to relate to others. For some people, separation from these early significant others does not occur and consequently has to be developed during therapy.

Therapy aims to reduce anxiety, using a positive relationship with the therapist to bring this about. Transference is used to examine the way that the patient relates to others. The unconscious fantasies which have their origins in infancy and affect the patient's perceptions of both self and others will also be explored.

Play therapy

This is based on work by Anna Freud (1952) and Melanie Klein. The idea is to allow earlier feelings and conflicts to emerge in children by using play as a means of communication. Play, as a method of uncensored communication, replaces the techniques of dream analysis and free association used with adults. Toys, such as people, cars, houses, animals, bricks and fences, are provided, along with drawing materials. Uncovering unconscious fantasies and the way that they distort present relationships is an important aim. Early object relations (e.g. between mother and child) can be detected and worked through in the course of transference, and simple interpretations communicated to the child (see Case study 3.4).

Case study 3.4: Kleinian play therapy (Rosenbluth 1974)

A four year old boy was referred for jealousy of his little sister, fussy eating and sleep disturbances. In therapy, he used animals to demonstrate his nightmares and how he saw the world. The pig was a 'good boy' and a smaller pig was his little sister. The tiger wanted to eat all the tame animals; although the boy was afraid of it, he hoped that it would eat the small pig.

The aggressive tiger was being used to represent both the therapist and the boy's mother, both of whom the boy feared. At times it also represented his own greed and needs for retaliation and control over the mother. The therapist interpreted all this for the boy, resulting in a reduction of the nightmares, but it took longer to lessen the boy's aggressiveness and to replace it with more affectionate impulses.

Psychoanalytically oriented psychotherapies

These aim to use a briefer, more focused form of psychoanalysis which hopefully deals with the presenting problem (the problem which causes the client to seek help) more quickly than classical psychoanalysis. Nowadays, this type of therapy is far more common than psychoanalysis and is available on the NHS, (for example, Strupp (1993) used a time-limited therapy which takes 25–30 sessions to complete). The analyst is more directive in focusing on areas directly relevant to a specific problem faced by the patient, and transference is not encouraged to develop. Current life and relationships will also be explored to a greater extent than in classical psychoanalysis. Many of these approaches are utilised by ego analysts such as Erik Erikson, who regard the ego as the key personality structure and aim to develop its potential to be constructive and creative in the course of therapy.

Psychodynamic group therapies

Both Jung and Adler (particularly the latter) accepted the importance of working with patients in groups. Suitable patients are those who are able and motivated to work within the group process. This means that they must have a certain amount of ego strength in order to cope with the interaction and the emotion generated. Free association in this context is replaced by free-floating discussion (i.e. discussion without censorship). Early relationships may be revealed by relationships with other group members as well as with the therapist, adding to the value of transference processes.

Evaluation of modern psychodynamic approaches

Modern psychodynamic theories and therapies have extended classical approaches in several useful ways, increasing their flexibility and availability. The use of these modern methods with groups, with children and over more limited periods of time has helped to make them more accessible. In particular, there is evidence (Koss and Butcher 1986) that such brief therapy may be no less effective than time-unlimited treatment. A study of brief analytic therapy by Sloane et al. (1975) found it to be as effective as behaviour therapy ; both were more effective than no treatment over a four-month period.

Applicability and evaluation

Psychoanalysis is best suited to well-educated, articulate neurotics, although it has been applied to other mental disorders to a lesser degree, and adapted for use with children and in group settings. However, it is a lengthy process in its original form, and its principles lack scientific support. Outcome studies of modern psychodynamic therapies have suggested that in some cases it may be as effective as other therapies.

Chapter summary

In this chapter we have outlined the main techniques employed by Freudian psychoanalysis to uncover and deal with unconscious conflicts. The therapy has been evaluated as best suited to YAVIS types. Its disadvantages are its duration and cost, the lack of scientific evidence for Freud's theories, and the bias evident in some of Freud's case studies. Research into its effectiveness has yielded conflicting evidence. Modern variations include Kleinian psychodynamic therapy, play therapy, psychoanalytically-oriented psychotherapy and psychodynamic group therapy. All of these have helped to make psychodynamic approaches more flexible and available, although their utility with the more severe disorders is still questionable.

Make a chart to show the similarities and differences between Freudian psychoanalysis and modern psychodynamic approaches to therapy.

Review exercise

Sample essay questions

1 Compare and contrast the psychoanalytic and somatic approaches used in the treatment of abnormal behaviour. (24 marks) [AEB, June 1990]

2 Critically discuss psychoanalytic explanations of abnormal behaviour, including the treatment involved. (24 marks)

[AEB, June 1988]

Further reading

Masson, J. (1988) *Against Therapy*, London: Collins. (An excellent critique of Freud – well-researched and readable.)

Dryden, W. (1990) *Individual Therapy: A Handbook*, Milton Keynes: Oxford University Press. (Contains concise chapters on different types of psychodynamic therapy.)

4

Behavioural therapies

General principles
Behaviour therapies
Behaviour modification techniques
Applicability and evaluation

General principles

Formation of behaviour disorders

Behavioural therapies are based on the assumption that mental disorders are maladaptive behaviours which have resulted from faulty learning. The case of Little Albert, given in Chapter 1, provides an example of the way that phobias may be learnt. The solution is therefore to unlearn the behaviours. Learning occurs through either association (classical conditioning) or through reinforcement (operant conditioning), and the therapies based on these are known as behaviour therapy and behaviour modification respectively. In both cases the focus is on the individual's present symptoms, not the historical causes of the problem.

Before we can explore the different types of therapy that have utilised these principles, it is essential to outline what is involved in the two types of conditioning. Note that in both cases what is being produced is *learning*, which can be defined as 'a relatively permanent change in behaviour that occurs as a result of experience'. This definition excludes behaviours that are the result of physical changes, either temporary states such as those induced by drugs, or permanent states such as those resulting from accidents (e.g. amputations). **Classical conditioning** procedures have been derived from Pavlov's studies of salivation in dogs in 1927. These showed that if a bell was rung just before food was presented, dogs would learn to salivate to the bell alone after a series of such trials. The reflex response of salivation had become associated with a new stimulus, i.e. the bell. The procedure is shown in diagrammatic form in Figure 4.1, which also shows the terms that Pavlov introduced for the different components of the conditioning process.

Learning in this situation depends on two principles: contiguous association (presenting the stimuli to be associated – the bell and the food, for example – close together in time); and the **law of exercise** (repetition of this pairing). The process also has other important characteristics. **Extinction** is the first of these, whereby omission of the unconditioned stimulus (e.g. food) leads eventually to the conditioned response no longer being shown. The second, **generalisation**, refers to the tendency to show a conditioned response to stimuli similar to the original conditioned stimulus (e.g. similar sounding bells). The last, **discrimination**, is the ability to learn not to generalise, but to respond only to one specific conditioned stimulus.

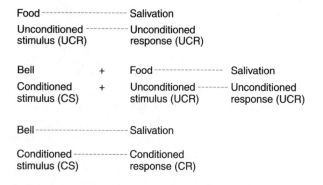

Figure 4.1   **The process of classical conditioning**

For the present purposes it is also important to note that although the phenomenon was originally demonstrated in dogs, this type of learning has also been shown to occur in humans. From the point of view of mental disorder, the most important reflex response is that of fear, since if this can be associated with new stimuli there are important implications for both the origins of disorders and for treatment.

Operant conditioning was originally termed 'instrumental conditioning' by the American psychologist Thorndike in 1913, and later renamed by its most famous theorist, Skinner (1938). The latter demonstrated that in a piece of apparatus called a Skinner box, (shown in Figure 4.2) a rat or pigeon would learn to press a lever or peck at a light in order to get a reward of food. It would learn to avoid behaviours that were followed by unpleasant consequences such as electric shocks. Therefore the consequences of these voluntary behaviours is what determines whether or not they will be repeated; this became known as the **law of effect**.

To increase the frequency of a behaviour (i.e. to **reinforce** it) there are two possibilities. The behaviour can be followed by positive consequences such as food (positive reinforcement), or by the omission of a negative event such as electric shock (negative reinforcement). It is also possible to decrease the frequency of behaviour by means of giving something unpleasant (**punishment**) or removing something pleasant (frustrative non-reward).

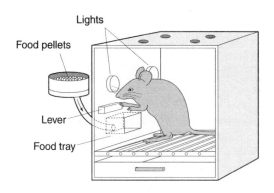

Figure 4.2   **A Skinner box**

Source: N. Hayes (1984) *A First Course in Psychology*, London: Harrap, p. 235

Insert the following terms into the correct places in the table below: positive reinforcement; negative reinforcement; punishment; frustrative non-reward.

	Stimulus given	Stimulus removed
Pleasant stimulus		
Unpleasant stimulus		

Look back over this section to check your answers.

As with classical conditioning, extinction can occur if reinforcement is omitted, and generalisation and discrimination have also been demonstrated. In the case of operant conditioning, generalisation and discrimination can extend or narrow the range of responses that are given as well as extending or narrowing the range of stimuli that are responded to. For example, instead of jumping on a lever as a response, a rat may reach up and pull it down with its paw.

Another important aspect of this type of conditioning is the possibility of **behaviour shaping**, whereby completely new behaviours can be developed gradually by rewarding any which are more similar to what is wanted. The animal will have to display something closer to the desired behaviour each time before it is rewarded, a process known as **successive approximation**.

See if you can make a list of the similarities and differences between classical and operant conditioning.

46

These processes have been specifically applied to the acquisition of mental disorder by Mowrer (1947) in his **two-factor model** of fear and avoidance. He suggested that fear of specific stimuli may be acquired through classical conditioning (first factor), so that a reflexive fear response becomes linked to new stimuli (such as spiders). This fear is unpleasant, so the individual learns to reduce it by avoiding the conditioned stimuli, which is an example of operant conditioning (second factor) through negative reinforcement. Such responses are extremely resistant to extinction (Solomon and Wynne 1954).

Maintenance of behaviour disorders

As the two-factor model implies, once maladaptive behaviour has been learnt it will be maintained only if the right conditions exist. Therefore treatment must be preceded by **functional analysis** to establish which conditions are responsible for maintaining the behaviour in question – including stimuli, prompts and reinforcers. To assist with this, the STAR system can be used as a guide. According to this, it is necessary to look at:

S – setting conditions (which environments prompt behaviour?)
T – triggers (which specific events prompt behaviour?)
A – antecedent events (any other events which occur before the behaviour?)
R – results (the consequences of the behaviour for the client)

This analysis allows the conditions to be changed in the course of therapy, hopefully leading to changes in the target behaviour. Goals for change will be set that aim to bring about change more or less quickly depending on the nature of the treatment used. The individual nature of this analysis means that such approaches are not generally appropriate for group work.

Behavioural theories have opened the door to a wide range of different therapies, which divide into two groups: behaviour therapies and behaviour modification techniques. These will be explored in the following sections.

Behaviour therapies

Behaviour therapies are based on classical conditioning. Four main approaches will be discussed here: systematic desensitisation; aversion therapy and covert sensitisation; exposure therapy (implosion and flooding); and positive conditioning.

Systematic desensitisation is based on the finding of Watson and Rayner (1920) that they could classically condition fear of a pet rat in an infant they called 'Little Albert', by making a loud noise whenever he was playing with the animal (see Chapter 1 for details). Subsequently, Jones (1925) found with a child he called 'Little Peter' that fears like this could be alleviated by associating the feared object instead with a pleasant response such as eating.

Wolpe (1958) developed this procedure into what he called **reciprocal inhibition**, using stronger antagonistic responses such as relaxation to overcome fear. It relied on the antagonistic response being stronger than the fear, and this was achieved in two ways. First, training was given in relaxation. Second, fear was introduced using a graded series of stimuli (known as an **anxiety hierarchy**), starting with the least fearful and only moving on to a more fearful stimulus when the current one was no longer frightening. An example of an anxiety hierarchy for examination phobia consists of a list of stimuli that evoke increasing amounts of anxiety, as follows:

1   A month before an examination
2   Two weeks before an examination
3   A week before an examination
4   Three days before an examination
5   One day before an examination
6   The night before an examination
7   Waiting for the examination paper to be given out
8   Waiting to go into the examination room.
9   Answering the examination paper
10 On the way to college on the morning of the examination

Wolpe began with 'in vivo' or real-life exposure, and moved on to use imaginary situations to further reduce the initial levels of fear. This became known as systematic desensitisation, and developed into a popular and successful treatment for phobias. For example, McGrath *et al.* (1990) found that it was effective for around 75 per cent of specific phobias (i.e. phobias in which fear can be related to a specific object or event, rather than a more general fear such as agoraphobia). Even with disorders such as agoraphobia, improvement has been found in 60–80 per cent of cases (Craske and Barlow 1993). A recent system introduced by Greist *et al.* (1997), called B. T. Steps, uses desensitisation procedures to provide self-treatment over the telephone for obsessive-compulsive disorder. Once registered by a specialist, the client is linked to a computerised system which establishes what triggers their fears and how severe the fears are. Goals can then be established (for example, not hand-washing for two hours after touching a toilet seat), and these can be gradually made more challenging until the fear is conquered. Such procedures have the advantage of being extremely cost-effective.

Aversion therapy, on the other hand, is used to increase the level of fear associated with carrying out unwanted behaviours, such as those occurring in substance abuse (which includes alcoholism, tobacco smoking and the use of psychoactive drugs) and sexual deviance. Alcoholism, for example, may be treated by administering an emetic (a drug that induces nausea and vomiting) as the unconditioned stimulus (UCS), just prior to alcohol consumption, the conditioned stimulus (CS). The nausea produced by the drug as a unconditioned response (UCR) eventually becomes a conditioned response (CR) to the CS of alcohol. The result is that alcohol will be avoided. In order to prolong the association, the **emetic** (such as 'Antabuse') can be inserted under the skin in a slow-release capsule.

The effectiveness of this procedure is generally found to be low. For example, Wallerstein (1957) found that only 24 per cent of a sample of alcoholics showed improvement one year after being given aversion therapy. However, it is important to remember that such disorders are notoriously difficult to treat by any method and the relapse rate is generally high.

Aversion therapy is less popular now because of ethical objections to the use of such unpleasant procedures. However, as Lang and Melamed (1969) have pointed out (see Case study 4.1), both costs and benefits need to be considered when taking ethics into account.

Case study 4.1: ethics and aversion therapy (Lang and Melamed 1969)

The patient was a one year old baby who had been referred for persistant, life-threatening vomiting for which doctors could find no discernible physical cause. The child was treated with aversion therapy by being given one-second electric shocks to the leg whenever it showed signs of vomiting. Vomiting stopped after two sessions of treatment, and body weight increased by 26 per cent in two weeks. After three weeks the child was discharged from hospital. After five months he was declared to be physically and psychologically normal.

A recent development in the treatment of alcoholism using aversion therapy takes account of the ethical objections raised. The system, called 'Smell, Swish and Spit' (SSS), requires patients to simply smell the alcohol, take a mouthful (swish) and spit it out again. This means that they feel ill, but as they do not swallow the alcohol, they do not vomit (Cannon *et al.* 1981).

Another variation of aversion therapy is called **covert sensitisation**, where thoughts of the unwanted behaviour (such as sexual deviance) are paired in the imagination with unpleasant consequences such as arrest (Cautela 1967). Whether this is as effective as the original procedure is uncertain, but it carries fewer ethical implications.

Exposure therapy relies on the principle of extinction, whereby repeated presentation of the CS without the UCS eliminates the CR. This does not normally happen in real life, because the individual avoids the object or situation concerned. If imagined contact is used (sometimes known as 'in vitro'), the process is referred to as **implosion**; if the contact is real (also known as 'in vivo'), the process is called **flooding**. As an example of the latter, Wolpe (1973) describes a case in which a girl with a phobia of cars was driven around for four hours until her fear had subsided. These procedures are fast and effective with problems such as phobias, but must be used with care because of the stress induced. In vivo procedures such as flooding are generally more effective with specific phobias than in vitro procedures such as implosion (Menzies and Clarke 1993).

Positive conditioning utilises classical conditioning principles to establish a response rather than to eliminate one. It was first devised by Mowrer and Mowrer (1938) to eliminate nocturnal **enuresis** (bedwetting), which they felt resulted from failure to associate a full bladder with waking up and emptying it. It is often referred to as the 'bell-and-pad' method, because the patient sleeps on a moisture-sensitive pad which sets off a bell (UCS) as soon as urination starts. This wakes (UCR) the patient, who then experiences contraction of the bladder sphincter. After several trials, bladder distension (CS) alone will lead to sphincter contraction (CR) preventing urination.

Write down one strength and one weakness for each of the methods described in the previous section.

Progress exercise

Behaviour modification techniques

These are based on operant conditioning principles. Four approaches will be discussed here: simple behaviour modification; token economies; stimulus satiation; and negative practice.

Simple behaviour modification relies on the use of reinforcement to shape behaviour into what is wanted, through the process of successive approximations. An example is given by Isaacs *et al.* (1960) outlined in Case study 4.2.

Case study 4.2: simple behaviour modification (Isaacs et al. 1960)

The patient was a forty year old catatonic schizophrenic who had not spoken for nineteen years. The therapist noticed that his impassive stare was altered when he saw a packet of chewing gum, and it was decided to use the gum as a reinforcer, as it was the only thing that the patient responded to positively. The patient was shown a piece of gum, and rewarded by being given the gum when he looked at it. Then the reward was only given when the patient moved his lips. This behaviour-shaping process continued with the patient being required to produce sounds, the word 'gum', and eventually other words. After six weeks the patient began to speak to the therapist sponta-neously.

Speech has similarly been induced in autistic children by Lovaas *et al.* (1977), using food as a reward. Positive reinforcers can also be used to help obese patients to lose weight and anorexics to gain it (Bachrach *et al.* 1965), rewards being given for reaching targets in both cases.

Note that where therapy aims to eliminate undesirable behaviours, it has been found that the use of extinction is more effective than the use of punishment (Crooks and Stein 1991). For example, temper tantrums in a child may be increased by the use of punishment if their purpose is to get attention. If the tantrums are ignored, on the other hand, the lack of attention (i.e. lack of reinforcement) will lead to extinction. This is called the 'time out' technique.

Token economies are operant systems that have been devised for use in institutions, where it is not always convenient for staff to administer rewards to individuals immediately after the target behaviour is performed. Since this is the time when rewards are most effective, Allyon and Azrin (1965, 1968) created a system whereby staff could instead give out tokens for target behaviours such as bed-making, dressing, washing, being sociable or eating with cutlery. These tokens can then be exchanged by patients at a later date or time for privileges such as watching television, trips out, or special foods (see Chapter 11 for more details of this study).

The approach has been used successfully in psychiatric hospitals with long-term psychotic and mentally retarded patients, and in residential homes for the elderly. Behaviours related to personal hygiene, tidiness, self-sufficiency and social interaction have been increased, and violent behaviour decreased. However, such approaches require trained staff to ensure consistency in the administration of reinforcements, and in many cases behaviours will not be maintained when tokens are withdrawn (e.g. if the patient leaves the hospital).

Stimulus satiation relies on the principle that most reinforcers lose their appeal if the individual has had enough of them. Allyon and Azrin (1965) used this principle to treat a case of psychotic stealing and towel hoarding, in which the patient used to wrap towels around herself until she could manage no more, then fill her bed and room with them. When nurses were encouraged to give her more, rather than take them away, she began to remove them herself eventually.

Negative practice similarly relies on the principle of overdoing the learned response, such as facial tics and stammering which will eventually extinguish as a result of fatigue (Yates 1958). Another study by Clark (1966) employed this approach to treat patients with **Tourette's Syndrome**, which is characterised by the inability to inhibit antisocial behaviours such as swearing. The patient was required to repeat his or her favourite obscenity aloud as many times as possible over a one-minute period, alternating with a one-minute rest period.

For each of the therapies described in the previous section, make a note of one type of disorder which the therapy has been used to treat.

Progress exercise

Applicability and evaluation

Applicability

Behavioural techniques are best suited to cases where there is a clearly identifiable observable behaviour that is predictable and related to environmental triggers. Marks (1981) concluded that such techniques were the most suitable treatment for about 25 per cent of non-psychotic disorders. The patient must be co-operative and well-motivated. The problems that respond best include: phobias, social skills deficits, obsessive-compulsive disorders, sexual disorders, maladaptive habits such as stammering and enuresis, eating disorders such as obesity, psychosomatic disorders, and problems associated with mental retardation. Psychotic and substance abuse disorders are less suitable on the whole, as are cases involving generalised anxiety. In the former, learning may not be sufficient to remove the disordered behaviour, because it is maintained by biological or social factors. In the latter group, treatment is difficult because specific behaviours or situations are difficult to target for treatment.

Evaluation

The major criticisms of behavioural approaches are that they are unethical and manipulative. As we have seen, the procedures used may be unpleasant in themselves. It has also been pointed out that decisions about which behaviours to change are made by the therapist, and this could be regarded as a form of social control. For this reason, modern practitioners involve patients more fully in the decision-making process, and goal-setting is more of a joint activity. There is still the problem that (like many somatic approaches) such treatments deal only with symptoms (overt behaviours) and not with causes. According to psychodynamic theorists, this should lead to symptom substitution; practitioners' opinions differ regarding the extent to which this occurs in practice. However, relapse when reinforcement is withdrawn is certainly an issue, as mentioned previously.

Although behavioural techniques are based on sound theories, some have pointed out that it is unclear whether the therapies were in fact derived from those theories or whether the theories were simply used as justification after the event (Malleson 1973). It is, in fact, difficult to predict, on the basis of theory alone, which therapy will be effective for which disorder.

The positive aspects of the therapies are that they are often very quick to produce changes, the changes are quite specific instead of affecting large areas of individual functioning, and everyday functioning is not likely to be disrupted while the treatment takes place.

1 State whether each of the following procedures is based on operant or classical conditioning: token economy; systematic desensitisation; aversion therapy; negative practice; exposure therapy; stimulus satiation.

2 State which therapy has been used to treat each of the following disorders: bed-wetting; communication problems in autistics; car phobia; alcoholism; stammering; violence in psychotic patients. Check your answers against the text.

Review exercise

Chapter summary

In this chapter we have looked at classical and operant conditioning, which are the basic principles underlying behavioural treatments. Behaviour therapies, based on classical conditioning, include systematic and covert desensitisation, aversion therapy and covert sensitisation, exposure therapies and positive conditioning. Behaviour modification techniques, based on operant conditioning, include simple behaviour modification, token economies, stimulus satiation, and negative practice. The application of these approaches has covered the whole spectrum of mental disorder, but they seem most suitable for neurotic disorders with clear environmental triggers. These therapies have the advantage of being fast-acting and specific in action, and they do not disrupt everyday life. Their disadvantages include the fact that they deal with symptoms rather than causes, that behaviour acquired in these ways may not generalise to other situations, and that the therapies often have only weak relationships with behavioural theories. These approaches have also been criticised on ethical grounds for being manipulative, and depriving patients of free will.

Sample essay questions

1   Discuss some of the therapeutic approaches which may help in the treatment of phobic patients. (24 marks)   [AEB, June 1987]
2   Describe and evaluate behavioural approaches used in the therapeutic treatment of abnormal behaviour. (24 marks)

[AEB, June 1989]

Further reading

O'Sullivan, G. (1990) 'Behaviour therapy', in W. Dryden, *Individual Therapy: A Handbook*, Milton Keynes: Oxford University Press. (Concise outline of the main principles.)

Toates, F. and Slack, I. (1990) 'Behaviourism and its consequences', in I. Roth (ed.), *Introduction to Psychology*, Hove: LEA. (Good readable background on behaviourist principles with plenty of critical evaluation.)

Watson, J. and Rayner, R. (1920) 'Conditioned emotional reactions', in R. Gross *Key Studies in Psychology*, London: Hodder & Stoughton, 1994. (The original study of Little Albert, together with critical commentary.)

5

Cognitive and cognitive-behavioural therapies

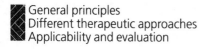

General principles
Different therapeutic approaches
Applicability and evaluation

General principles

Theories

As early as the 1940s Tolman's work on learning had suggested that a purely behaviourist view (as described in the previous chapter) was not sufficient because it ignored the contribution of thought processes to learning. Tolman began to talk of 'purposive behaviour' and 'expectations', both of which terms emphasise the importance of thoughts and perceptions (i.e. cognition) in determining behaviour. For example, a study by Tinkelpaugh (1928) showed that if a monkey that was accustomed to receive a banana as a reward had a piece of lettuce substituted instead while its attention was distracted, it showed unmistakable signs of frustration, appearing to look for the banana and sometimes shrieking at the experimenter.

In 1965, Bandura started to develop **social learning theory**, which emphasised learning by observation and imitation. He also demonstrated that learning could be 'stored up' for future use rather than being shown in behaviour immediately (known as **latent learning**). All of these processes imply that cognition is a crucial factor in learning.

Therapies

In the sphere of therapy, Rachman and Hodgson (1980) proposed a **three systems approach**, whereby psychological problems could be seen as having behavioural, cognitive/affective and physiological components. This encouraged researchers to explore areas other than overt behaviour. Cognitive-behavioural therapy (CBT) resembles behaviour therapy with its focus on the present rather than the past. It also makes the general assumption that interaction with the world is carried out via a process of interpretations and inferences about the things that happen to us. These cognitive processes can become distorted, but they are accessible to consciousness and the individual has the power to change them. For example, anorexics can be seen to be mis-perceiving (overestimating) their body size; depressives as focusing too much on their failures.

As well as distortions, people with mental disorders are prone to negative automatic thoughts which they cannot control, e. g. 'I never do anything right'. Underlying the distortions and disturbances in content is a cognitive schema (or mental structure) which is biased and rigid, and manipulates input to fit in with its view. For example, positive events or successes may be filtered out to fit in with the view of the self as a failure.

Aims

Thus the three aims of cognitive therapy are:

- to relieve symptoms and resolve problems
- to help the client to develop coping strategies
- to help the client to change underlying schemas (thereby preventing relapse)

According to Teasdale (1997) the important feature may be to teach the client *meta-awareness*, which is the ability to think about their own thoughts. Thoughts and feelings are seen as mental events that can be examined objectively and changed if necessary, rather than unchangeable components of the self, or facts to be accepted. These aims are achieved by teaching the client to monitor thought processes and then to test them against reality.

Steps

According to Beck and Emery (1985), there are four steps in doing this:

1   Conceptualisation of the patient's problems – what is at the root of them? For example, what is presented as fatigue due to stress could be due to negative thoughts about the self and relationships.
2   Choosing a therapeutic strategy. These will vary according to the nature of the client and the preferences of the therapist; the most commonly used are:

- *Distancing and distraction.* The client is encouraged to be an objective observer of his/her own thoughts, and to see them as if from a distance. This strategy helps to reduce the strength of negative feelings about them. Distraction is a technique for reducing the frequency of maladaptive thoughts by encouraging the client to think of something else whenever they occur.
- *Challenging automatic thoughts.* Their validity can be challenged by getting the client to carry out an experiment to test these thoughts, or by looking for evidence for and against them. Is it true, for example, that everything the client says or does is wrong?
- *Challenging underlying assumptions.* Again, this can be done by setting up an experiment, or by explaining the advantages and disadvantages of an assumption. Is it advantageous to consider yourself worthless or of no use to anyone, for example?
- *Building skills.* Skills such as assertiveness, time management and social skills may be lacking and can be taught (using role play, for example).

3 Choosing a technique. There are several possibilities, many of which are derived from behavioural approaches. Examples include:

- *Socratic questioning* (looking for evidence that supports or challenges beliefs)
- *Identifying negative automatic thoughts* (including teaching the client to observe and record them)
- *Modifying negative automatic thoughts.* These could be challenged by: reality testing to see if there is any evidence to support them; looking for alternatives; looking for alternative explanations; re-attribution (where a different explanation is given for the behaviour); decatastrophising (where the client is asked to think of the worst thing that could happen, and its consequences, which may not turn out to be so terrible after all); and looking at the advantages and disadvantages of a particular course of action. Behavioural techniques could include: relaxation; graded assignments; experiments; ratings of mastery and pleasure obtained from tasks; activity scheduling to encourage participation and action, rather than constant thinking and worrying; role play and rehearsal of new behaviours; and awareness training (making clients aware of their present bodily and thought processes, and raising the issues of choice and control).

4 Assessing the effectiveness of the technique. This is an important part of the process, and will be dealt with more fully in Chapters 8 and 10. The point is to acknowledge that every client is different, and may therefore respond in different ways.

Progress exercise

Summarise in table form the main theoretical principles, aims, steps and strategies used in cognitive therapy.

Different therapeutic approaches

Specific therapists have different approaches based on their own theoretical backgrounds. To give you some idea of the variation, we will here consider Beck, Ellis, Meichenbaum, Kelly and Bandura.

Beck (1967): Automatic thought treatment

Beck originated many of the strategies and techniques outlined in the previous section. In his work on depression he identified the importance of **cognitive distortions** and negative automatic thoughts (such as 'I am a failure'). Four types of these are (Beck *et al.* 1979):

arbitrary inference	making interpretations of situations, events or experiences in ways for which there is no factual evidence; the interpretation is such that it indicates low self-esteem
selective abstraction	focusing on details taken out of context and forming conclusions based on these only, ignoring other information
overgeneralisation	drawing a general conclusion from a single instance
magnification and minimisation	either over- or underestimating the importance of an event

These distortions can be seen as leading to the **cognitive triad** of depression – a negative view of the self (I am worthless), current experience (everything looks bleak, I cannot cope) and the future (nothing will ever get better). Such catastrophising beliefs can be challenged in therapy. For example, a depressed student may be led, by questioning, to the conclusion that they have in fact always done well in exams and should therefore have no difficulty in getting the grades required for university entrance.

Although mainly applied to depression, this approach has also been used in the treatment of phobias, anxiety and personality disorders (Beck and Emery, 1985, Beck and Freeman, 1990), and to eating disorders (Andrews 1991). It usually requires fifteen to twenty one-hour sessions over a period of three months. Rush *et al.* (1977) found that, of a sample of depressed patients treated with Beck's cognitive therapy for twelve weeks, 79 per cent were much improved, compared with 20 per cent of a drug treatment group. This difference was maintained at follow-up. (See Case study 5.1.)

Case study 5.1: Philippa (Moorey 1990)

Philippa was a forty-five year-old librarian who sought help for tension and anxiety. It emerged that she was low in self-esteem and felt that her mother was critical of her. Frequent negative thoughts included 'I'll never amount to anything'. During therapy, distancing was promoted by getting her to monitor situations and the negative thoughts associated with them. When the thoughts were challenged she was able to see that many of them derived from her misinterpretation of events. For example, she thought that her husband was angry with her for making mistakes, but in fact she was far more upset about the mistakes than he was. Asking her to provide evidence for other negative thoughts (such as 'I really don't matter'), showed that there was more evidence against than for them.

Her husband was brought in for some sessions, in which he was encouraged to be more openly supportive of her and less likely to dismiss her reactions as irrational. After ten sessions she showed improved self-esteem and reduced tension, and therapy was terminated.

Ellis (1962, 1991): Rational-emotive therapy

Another type of cognitive restructuring stems from the work of Ellis, who argued that people who suffer from mental disorders have irrational beliefs which lead to inappropriate emotions such as depression and guilt. If they develop instead a dispute system to challenge these beliefs, they will no longer suffer such emotional problems. For example, they may assume that they receive no social invitations because no-one likes them; a more likely explanation is that they are often busy, or do not issue such invitations themselves. Some examples of irrational beliefs, and their rational alternatives, are given in the following table:

Irrational belief	Rational belief
I must be perfect	I need to be realistic rather than to strive for perfection
Life is awful when things go wrong	When things go wrong I can make the best of the situation
I must obtain love and approval from significant others	Love and approval are nice, but not essential

In Ellis' **ABC model**, activating events (A) or obstacles lead to beliefs (B) about those events, which may be rational or irrational. These in turn lead to emotional and behavioural consequences (C). The nature of the beliefs determines the nature of the consequences, as Figure 5. 1 shows.

A   **Activating event/obstacle**
(e.g. not receiving many social invitations)

B   **Rational belief**   **Irrational belief**
(perhaps I haven't shown   (nobody likes me)
much interest in others)

C   **Desirable**   **Undesirable**
emotion/behaviour   **emotion/behaviour**
(demonstrate disappointment   (feel upset and ignore
and interest)   other people)

Figure 5.1   **The ABC model**

Draw up an ABC model, as shown in Fig 5. 1, for the event/obstacle 'being unemployed'.

In rational-emotive therapy (RET) the therapist is active and directive to a greater degree than in Beck's Cognitive Restructuring. Homework may be given in the form of behavioural experiments. It has been usefully applied to treat anxiety, anger, depression and anti-social behaviour (Haaga and Davison 1993), but is less effective with disorders such as anxiety and agoraphobia. The main criticism is that some 'irrational' beliefs are in fact more accurate than those of most people, a phenomenon known as 'depressive realism', or the 'sadder but wiser' effect. For example, depressives give more accurate estimates of the likelihood of disaster than do controls (Alloy and Abramson 1979). This implies that actually defining what constitutes an irrational belief could be a problem.

Meichenbaum's self-instructional training (1976)

This approach suggests that behaviour change can be brought about if clients are encouraged to change the instructions they give them-selves, in the form of 'self-talk', to more adaptive versions. These internal dialogues are externalised during therapy and discussed, then coping strategies are developed to deal with them. These strategies include relaxation, sub-vocal instruction (such as telling yourself to 'stop!' the thoughts, called 'thought-stopping'), and role-playing plans. Self-instructions are especially important in coping with stressful situations, and have led Meichenbaum to develop 'stress inoculation training'. In this procedure, people are first asked how they think in stressful situations – for example, they may say 'I can't cope'. They are then encouraged to develop and practise more positive self-statements such as 'worrying won't help', 'one step at a time' and 'it could be worse', and reinforcing self-statements such as 'that was better'.

As well as being used in industry for stress management, such procedures have been applied to the treatment of test and speech anxiety, phobias, schizophrenia, and hyperactivity in children.

Kelly (1955): personal construct therapy

This theory has led to the formulation of therapies which can be seen as broadly cognitive in their approach, although Kelly is regarded by some as a humanistic psychologist because of his emphasis on the importance of experience and individuality. According to Kelly, our view of the world and of ourselves is coloured by our personal constructs, i.e. the concepts which we use to make sense of the world, such as 'good–bad'. These will be maintained as long as they seem to give an accurate prediction of what to expect. People who need therapy are 'stuck' with inappropriate constructs, and need to be helped to find alternative ways of evaluating themselves and their problems. A wide variety of techniques may be used in personal construct theory to help them to do this, a selection of which are outlined below:

Techniques used in personal construct therapy

1 *The repertory grid* is a procedure for finding out what constructs the client uses and how the client views him/herself and others. It is useful for monitoring change over time.
2 *Laddering*. The client is asked to explain constructs at a progressively more abstract level. For example, a preference for friendly rather than aggressive people may be explained on the basis that friendly people are less likely to attack the client; if the client is then asked to explain why being attacked is a problem, she may say that she doesn't know how to handle the situation.
3 *ABC model*. The client is asked to explain the advantages and disadvantages of each pole of a construct. Taking the example of aggressive versus friendly again, aggressive behaviour may have the advantage of not being picked on by others but the disadvantage of discouraging friendships; friendly behaviour would show the opposite pattern.

4   *Self characterisation*. The client is asked to write a character sketch as if he/she were the main character in a play.

5   *Fixed-role therapy*. The therapist uses the fixed-role sketch to write another version which has been modified, until the client feels that it describes a person he could potentially be. The client then has to enact this fixed role for a few weeks. The idea of this is to convince the client that change is possible and that this will produce different responses in others.

The applicability of this approach to therapy depends very much on the resourcefulness of the therapist. Verbal fluency in the client and shared cultural expectations between therapist and client are helpful. In practice, withdrawn schizophrenics or violent clients will be difficult to deal with. In general, it is not applicable to group therapy, although there are some examples of its use in this context (e.g. Beail and Parker 1991). (See Case study 5.2.)

Case study 5.2: Rowena (Fransella 1990)

Rowena was a thirty-five year old unmarried career woman who had a problem with establishing lasting relationships with the opposite sex. Her self-characterisation was that she was warm and loving with a desire for a family and a fear of being alone. In therapy it was hypothesised that early rejection by her mother had led her to see herself as a rejected person. This in turn had encouraged the development of behaviour patterns likely to lead to rejection, such as smothering men with love at too early a stage in the relationship.

When the opportunity arose in the form of a new relationship, she was encouraged to experiment with new behaviours, such as letting the man set the pace. After ten sessions she terminated therapy, because the new relationship appeared to be a success.

Bandura's modelling (1969, 1977)

This relies on the use of the social learning principles of observation and imitation. The client will be presented with a model (live or filmed) who is behaving in the desired ways, and encouraged to imitate this behaviour. Reinforcement will be given for appropriate imitations. The cognitive aspect of the therapy is the client's mental representation of the behaviour which has been observed. It is this which leads to imitation, and thence to reinforcement. For example, a client with snake phobia may be shown a model playing with a snake and allowing it to twine itself around their body. Bandura (1971) claimed that this procedure succeeded in eliminating fear in every case where it was used. As well as phobias, it has been applied to social skills training, assertiveness, and reduction of aggressive behaviour (e.g. in violent criminals). Bandura considers that the procedure works primarily because it increases feelings of self-efficacy – the feeling of being in control, capable of effective action and able to cope.

For each of the therapies mentioned, note one key technique and one type of disorder that it can be used to treat.

Progress exercise

Applicability and evaluation

Applicability

Cognitive therapy has been applied to a wide range of disorders since it was initiated for the treatment of depression. Phobias, panic attacks (see Clark *et al.* 1992, in Chapter 11), eating disorders, generalised anxiety, stress, sexual problems and antisocial behaviours have all received attention. For such disorders cognitive therapy is at least as effective as drugs (Hollon *et al.* 1992), and is associated with a lower relapse rate in long-term follow-up studies (Evans *et al.* 1992).

THERAPEUTIC APPROACHES IN PSYCHOLOGY

James and Blackburn (1995), however, have shown that cognitive therapy is less useful with obsessive-compulsive disorder. The more long-term and severe the disorder (especially if it involves hallucinations and delusions), the less likely it is to respond to cognitive challenges. Nevertheless, Haddock (1998) has reported that cognitive therapy may be an effective treatment for hallucinations in recently diagnosed (as opposed to long-term) schizophrenics. Within the normal range, intelligence of the client does not appear to be a problem, although clients must be capable of gaining some insight into their problems. Couple and group therapies may also have some potential.

Evaluation

Cognitive therapies are cost-effective because they do not usually involve prolonged treatment. They are becoming popular with the NHS, although the lack of trained therapists means that they are still not widely available. They are popular with clients who do not wish to delve too deeply into their hidden fears, and would therefore avoid psychodynamic approaches.

However, cognitive therapies have been criticised, like behavioural approaches, for focusing on symptoms rather than causes. It has been argued that by providing clients with strategies for self-help, they are less manipulative than behavioural treatments. Nevertheless, it is clear that the therapist is still making judgements concerning which thoughts are acceptable, so ethical considerations cannot be dismissed entirely.

Chapter summary

This chapter has dealt with therapeutic approaches based on the view that mental disorder results from faulty cognitions, which can be corrected in therapy. Beck's automatic thought treatment is based on the elimination of negative thought, and has proved to be a successful treatment for depression. Ellis' rational-emotive therapy, which aims to deal with the irrational thoughts that lead to inappropriate emotions and behaviours, works well with depression, anger and anti-social behaviours. Meichenbaum's self-instructional training uses self-talk to help with stress, anxieties and hyperactivity. Kelly's personal construct therapy aims to adjust the client's constructs, or interpretation of the world. Bandura's modelling procedure uses demonstrations and role play of desirable behaviours to increase self-efficacy, and has been used for social skills training and phobic clients. Cognitive-behavioural therapies in general are cost-effective and popular with clients who prefer logic to emotion-based approaches, but they are not entirely devoid of ethical problems.

Link each of the theorists listed on the left with one of the therapies on the right:

(1) Beck   (a) Self-instructional training
(2) Ellis   (b) Automatic thought treatment
(3) Kelly   (c) Modelling
(4) Meichenbaum   (d) Personal construct therapy
(5) Bandura   (e) Rational-emotive therapy

Check your answers in the text.

Review exercise

Sample essay question

Discuss the use of any two cognitive-behavioural therapies in the treatment of depression. (24 marks)   [AEB, June 1998]

ther reading

Blackburn, I. (1984) 'Cognitive approaches to clinical psychology', in J. Nicholson and H. Beloff (eds) *Psychology Survey*, vol. 5, BPS. (Excellent coverage of basic principles and a range of approaches.)

Prentice, P. (1995) 'Rational-Emotive Therapy', *Psychology Review* 2 (2) November 1995, 28–31. (Concise coverage of a therapeutic approach neglected by many other texts.)

6

Humanistic and socio-cultural therapies

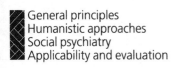

General principles
Humanistic approaches
Social psychiatry
Applicability and evaluation

General principles

After psychoanalysis and behaviourism, humanistic psychology has been described as the 'third force' in psychology. Its view of mental disorder as resulting from blocking of the individual's potential for personal growth means that most of the therapies have the aim of removing such blocks and helping clients to become aware of their real selves. Although the various therapies have markedly different ways of achieving this, certain common themes can be discerned as follows:

1   The importance of subjective experience (including feelings, thoughts and bodily processes) and the holistic nature of that experience.
2   The universal existence of the capacity for personal growth and personal agency (i.e. making choices and taking responsibility for self-direction).

3   The importance of purposive meaning in each person's life (Frankl 1959), and the potential for achieving this through actions (especially creative ones), aesthetic experiences, and loving relationships.

4   The importance of the right conditions for the development of the self-concept (Rogers 1959).

5   The need for self-actualisation (the realisation of one's potential) and the relevance of peak experiences (moments of enlightenment) and altered states of consciousness (such as meditation) in achieving this (Maslow 1954).

6   The importance of joy as part of our emotional experience.

7   Authenticity. The existentialists in particular emphasise the importance of establishing a unique self-identity and living in what they refer to as an authentic way. By this they mean getting to know and understand yourself and the environment in which you live, and developing your own purpose in life.

As with many of the other therapeutic approaches discussed so far (particularly psychodynamic therapies), the humanistic theories often appear to have developed from the therapies rather than vice-versa. In some instances, the links between theory and practice are not strong. In general, they share the aim of increasing the client's self-knowledge and authenticity, with personal growth and eventual self-actualisation hopefully following from this. The way that this aim is achieved is extremely diverse, and the therapies which follow should be regarded as a selection of the most widely used and/or acclaimed rather than a comprehensive list.

Humanistic approaches

Rogers' person-centred therapy (1959)

The aim of this approach is to facilitate personal growth through the relationship between the therapist and the client. The focus is very much on the present rather than the past. Of all the therapies, this is the least directive, because Rogers felt that true personal growth would only occur when people became more able to think through problems and make decisions for themselves. The therapist's role is that of an 'active listener' who provides an atmosphere of trust and warmth in which growth can occur. Many mental disorders are felt to result from the client's self-concept being threatened by demands from others which are incongruent with that self-concept. For example, an intelligent person may have their self-development blocked because parental expectations are that they should remain at home and not go away to university. Only in the context of a warm, understanding and non-evaluative relationship will the client feel sufficiently free from threat to be himself and grow. According to Rogers this atmosphere is dependent on the provision of three core conditions; in their presence therapeutic change will be almost inevitable. They are outlined below.

Core conditions for person-centred therapy

1   *Genuineness* (also termed **authenticity** or congruence) is the most important, and refers to the need for the therapist to behave as an ordinary person would, rather than taking on the role of a detached, white-coated clinician. This requires the therapist to be aware of his/her own thoughts and feelings and to be able to communicate these to the client if it is necessary to do so. Any falseness, Rogers felt, would be detected by the client, who would then be less likely to trust the therapist. Honesty is therefore important, but at the same time the therapist's feelings should not be imposed on the client.

2   **Unconditional positive regard** is a process whereby clients can be made to feel that they are being accepted without reservation for what they are. They must feel secure and liked, and it is important that this liking, unlike any which they may have received from others, is not dependent on what they say or do.

3   *Empathic understanding* was felt by Rogers to be more trainable than the other core conditions. It is the ability to see the world from the client's perspective and to understand how the client is feeling. It is different to sympathy, which is an expression of concern about those feelings. This relies to some extent on the process of checking understanding with the client using the technique of reflection, whereby statements are summarised and fed back to the client for checking (e.g. 'Is this what you mean?' or 'So you are saying that…').

Given these conditions, the client's self-concept should become more congruent; that is to say, it should become more positive, and behaviour should change to become more in line with it. According to Frick (1971), the following changes can be perceived:

moving away from:	keeping up appearances; 'shoulding', i.e. responding to externally imposed obligations, and the expectations of others
moving towards:	valuing honesty and acceptance of the self and associated feelings; self-direction; a focus on the present rather than the past or the future; greater understanding of others and a desire for greater intimacy in relationships; greater openness to all experiences

One of Rogers' best-known case studies is summarised below.

Case study 6.1: Mrs Oak (Rogers 1961)

Mrs Oak was a housewife in her late thirties who came for therapy because she was having difficulties with marital and family relationships. Early in therapy (the fifth interview) she reported that she was becoming more consciously aware of her current experiences and dwelling less on her problems. Rogers regards that as a characteristic shift in therapy. 'It may be represented schematically as the client's feeling that "I came here to solve problems, and now I find myself just experiencing myself".'

By the thirtieth interview, Mrs Oak reported that she had become aware of the positive warmth and interest of the therapist, a factor which she referred to after a therapy session as the most outstanding experience of all, as she had previously found it difficult to accept positive feelings from others. As she puts it, this in turn 'permits me to realise that I care, and care deeply, for and about others'. In the thirty-third interview, this led to another important development, the acceptance of herself as she is, and further, a liking for herself. By the thirty-fourth interview, near the end of therapy, she states: 'It seems to me to really be a way of – of not – of finding yourself in a place where you aren't forced to make rewards and you aren't forced to punish. It is – it means so much. It just seems to me to make for a kind of freedom'.

Evaluation

Rogerian therapy helps clients to develop their own decision-making skills and leaves the responsibility for this with them. Clients are not told what to do by the therapist. The non-intrusive nature of the therapy makes it one of the most ethical forms of treatment available. It has been applied to many other spheres where intervention is required, as well as to mental disorder. In the form of counselling, it has been extended to career choice, to the workplace, to bereavement and breastfeeding counselling, and has been used by groups such as the Samaritans. It has been used for marriage guidance with couples and for treating people in groups (known as 'encounter groups' – Rogers 1970). Its use with groups not only saves the therapist's time, it also allows clients to learn from one another.

When used to treat mental disorder, even Rogers felt that his form of therapy worked best with people whose adjustment to life was reasonably sound. Although it has been applied to severe disorders such as schizophrenia, it may not be the most appropriate treatment in those cases, somatic therapy being a more likely choice. Rigid, authoritarian people who need to be given structure and direction, and people who are focused on logic rather than on emotion may also find it hard to benefit.

The therapy has been criticised by several writers who feel that it is ultimately based on the use of positive reinforcement and is therefore simply a form of behaviour therapy. Truax (1966), for example, pointed out that Rogers tended to show unconditional positive regard when clients made statements indicative of progress. Other critics feel that the safe atmosphere provided by the therapist could be regarded as an unrealistic situation which is unobtainable in the context of everyday life. (The obvious rejoinder to this – see, for example, Smail

(1987) – is that it is everyday life which needs the adjustment!) The view that all people are naturally good and worthy of unconditional positive regard is also difficult to accept in some cases, e.g. antisocial personality disorder.

Outcome research indicates that counselling has been effective in truancy cases (Rose and Marshall 1974) and in medical practice (Ashurst and Ward 1983). Mitchell (1977) examined the importance of the three core conditions and found that genuineness was the key aspect in the sense that when it was lacking, warmth and empathy were less effective. However, Parloff *et al.* (1978) found that outcome was not related to therapist genuineness and empathy.

Progress exercise

In what ways does Rogerian therapy illustrate the common themes of humanistic and existential therapies outlined at the beginning of this chapter?

Berne's transactional analysis (1964)

This is based on the concept of ego states, which can take one of three forms: the Parent (upholder of society's prohibitions), Child (impulsive and pleasure-seeking) or Adult (rational state). Our behaviour is determined by the ego state that we are in at any given time, and the ego state itself may be altered according to the social interaction we are engaging in. Different ego states can be used manipulatively to play 'games' in the way that we interact with others. For example, taking the role of the child may be done deliberately to make the other person play the role of the parent. If one ego state becomes dominant, mental disorder may result.

The aim of **transactional analysis** (TA) is to attain social control by developing the adult ego state. Work is carried out in groups to teach clients how to recognise and understand the ego states and how these may be used during 'games' to obtain 'strokes' (attention) from others.

Another feature of TA is **script analysis**. Scripts are the overall strategies people use for playing out their lives. Developed in early life, these may no longer be appropriate later on, and increasing awareness of their existence can help individuals to modify them.

Evaluation

Although based on psychoanalysis, TA places more emphasis on the here and now. There is little if any outcome research, but it is a popular approach, particularly in the USA, with individuals who are not severely mentally disordered. Since it involves group work to analyse communication difficulties, it can be seen as a forerunner to conjoint therapy, discussed in a later section.

Perls' gestalt therapy (1969)

In the belief that mental disorder is the result of a blocking of aware-ness, the aim of this form of therapy is to develop greater awareness of self and a sense of wholeness (which is what the word 'gestalt' means). The focus is very much on the present (or 'here and now') but the ther-apist in this case is very directive. Perls objected to the use of techniques, calling them 'gimmicks', and possibly because of this a very wide range has been employed. Typically, therapy occurs in a group setting, with the focus being on each individual in turn. The aim is to make each person aware of who they are and what they are feeling, and to encourage each to accept responsibility for their deci-sions, actions and feelings (known as 'owning' them). Drama is used, in the form of role play for example, where people may act out both sides of a relationship in turn. This could involve the use of the '**empty chair technique**', where the client first addresses a chair in which the other party is imagined to be sitting, and then moves into the chair to play the role of the other party. Awareness is increased by asking the client to use the first person when speaking about things, e.g. 'I think that…' instead of 'It seems that…'. Amplification, or exaggeration of feelings, may also be used in order to make the client more aware of them. These techniques can then be used independently by the clients, so that they can maintain their increased levels of awareness.

Evaluation

Although gestalt therapy has been extremely popular, especially in the USA, there have been few studies of its effectiveness. These would be very difficult to carry out, as with many of the other therapies in this group, because the aims and methods are so diverse and very much tailored to the individual. It is likely that it will be more acceptable to some types of people than others; some would shrink from emotional, dramatic group encounters of this kind.

Progress exercise

See if you can answer the following questions:

1 What were Rogers' 'core conditions'?
2 What were Berne's three ego states?
3 What is meant by the 'empty chair'?
4 Name one strength and one weakness of the therapies of Rogers, Berne and Perls.

Check your answers in the text before you read on.

Social psychiatry

Conjoint (family) therapy

Conjoint therapy refers to therapy where the family members are together in sessions with a therapist, a procedure which involves treating the immediate family group of the identified client as a unit. The approach was initiated by the finding that patients treated in hospital often relapse when returned to their home environment, suggesting that the problems shown by the client may be a reflection of the way that the family functions as a whole. Change in the family may therefore be more important than change in the client.

The goal of this form of therapy is to increase understanding of the problems caused by the way family members interact, and to make that interaction more harmonious (Gurman *et al*. 1986). The approach can be adapted to suit many different theoretical models (e.g. psychodynamic), but is particularly associated with the phenomenological theories.

Following the work of Jackson and Weakland (1961) and Bateson *et al.* (1956), the ways in which family members interact are analysed to identify faulty communication patterns and difficult relationships, e.g. who speaks to whom, who is dominant and who is dependent. Both verbal and non-verbal communications will be analysed to assist with this. Barriers, misunderstandings or overdependence between family members can then be detected and adjusted.

Change can be brought about in a variety of ways, drawing on a range of theoretical models. For example, homework tasks may be given which aim to increase interaction with a particular family member. 'Caring days' may be introduced, whereby husband and wife take it in turns to devote themselves to the other for a day (Stuart 1976). Reinforcement of the other is important, as is cognitive change in order to develop skills in problem-solving and conflict reduction. Listening skills and techniques for clarifying what the other has said will also be useful.

Evaluation

Initially introduced for work with families of schizophrenics, family therapy has been used more recently to treat sexual problems (LoPiccolo and Freidman 1985) and anorexia (Rosman *et al.* 1976). A meta-analysis of the results of twenty studies (Hazelrigg *et al.* 1987) indicates that it is beneficial for many types of problem. According to Gurman *et al.* (1986) it is more successful than individual therapy for marital problems, and has proved useful with schizophrenia and agoraphobia. It is generally more useful with younger couples.

Milieu therapy

Introduced by Jones (1953), this was based on the argument that the social milieu of institutions needed to change if patients were to improve. An example is provided by Cooper (1967) in his report on Villa 21. The ward, within a large mental hospital, was developed into a community where no distinctions were made between patients (or residents) and staff, and decisions were made jointly in community meetings. The aim was to reduce feelings of institutionalisation and increase the residents' self-respect and feelings of responsibility.

Evaluation

Most such experiments were relatively short-lived; Villa 21, for example, ran for four years. According to Cooper (1967) further development was prevented by the constraints of the institution, but the way was paved for the establishment of such units within the community. 'A step forward means ultimately a step out of the mental hospital into the community'. A summary of Cooper's report is presented in Case study 6.2.

Case study 6.2: family and milieu therapy with schizo-phrenics (Cooper 1967)

Forty-two schizophrenics were treated by family and milieu therapy with reduced use of tranquillisers and no other somatic or individual therapy. The average length of stay in hospital was three months, all being discharged within one year of admission. Of these, 17 per cent were re-admitted within 1 year of discharge. Of those not re-admitted, 70 per cent were able to support themselves.

Therapeutic communities

Places such as Kingsley Hall and the Arbours Association were set up by Laing (1960) and Cooper (1967) with the aim of providing a safe environment in which their clients could continue their 'voyage of self-discovery', which is what their mental disorder was considered to be. Therapists and clients lived communally, and explored the experiences of the clients together, with a view to encouraging development in new directions. The style adopted by the therapist was variable, since flexibility was regarded to be one of the keys to successful treatment. The therapist needed to shed all preconceptions (hence this is very much an existential approach) and abandon all attempts to change the client. Through conversation, the client's view of the world was revealed, identifying their basic assumptions and self-deceptions and creating awareness of the limitations of the human condition and the implications of personal decisions. The client should then be able to come to terms with what cannot be changed and to tackle what can be changed.

Evaluation

Such experimental communities have been rare, and have not been subject to rigorous evaluation. The success stories (e.g. the case of Mary Barnes, who went on to become a successful artist) have received more publicity than the less successful cases. One problem with evaluation is that there is no clear end-point for such therapy, as there is no criterion for a cure; it is therefore difficult to decide whether the therapy has been successful for a given individual or not. An outcome study by Rosser *et al.* (1987) found in a five-year follow-up of patients that 90 per cent had obtained employment.

Applicability and evaluation

Most people are likely to show benefits from these approaches, although some may be more suitable for certain types of personality than others (e.g. gestalt therapy may suit those with outgoing personalities). Rogerian therapy has mainly found its niche with neurotics and those who are reasonably well-adjusted, whilst therapeutic communities catered mainly for schizophrenics; hence the whole spectrum of disorders has been tackled with varying degrees of success. In general such approaches are best suited to those who want to challenge the ways of the world and feel alienated from it, or those trying to cope with major changes such as bereavement. Verbal ability is not important, but commitment to the pursuit of meaning is (van Deurzen-Smith 1990).

Many writers feel that such therapies are fundamentally selfish in that they encourage personal growth at the expense of others. In this respect, although they embrace Eastern philosophies, they can be seen as typically Western in outlook. Others consider them too far detached from the real world to be of much use. The extent of social pressures, for example, means that for many people free will is an illusion. Other problems relate to the debate about the effectiveness of therapy. Without agreement on what constitutes a cure, this is difficult to assess, as mentioned in the previous section. Beyond these issues, however, is the problem of whether science can provide the measures appropriate for what these therapists feel is meaningful about the changes they observe in therapy (Yalom 1980).

Chapter summary

In this chapter we have looked at the common themes shared by this diverse group of therapies. They all emphasise understanding the world from the viewpoint of the individual client, and increasing the client's self-knowledge and personal development.

Rogers' person-centred therapy has three core conditions and aims to increase the congruence between the client's perceived self and ideal self. It has formed the basis of the counselling movement. Perls' gestalt therapy aims to increase self-awareness and sense of wholeness, and is popular with the more outgoing types of patient. Berne's transactional analysis aims to develop more appropriate ways of relating to others through the analysis of ego states. Social psychiatry takes the emphasis away from the individual with the use of conjoint (family), milieu and community therapies. Their aim is to improve the quality of the social environment to facilitate the client's development.

Such approaches are useful with certain types of individual, rather than particular types of disorder. There is little outcome research, but some critics feel that these therapies are too detached from the real world and that they encourage selfishness.

Review exercise

Draw up a table to show, for the humanistic and social psychiatry approaches separately, examples of therapy, strengths and weaknesses.

Sample essay questions

(a) Describe some assumptions of the humanistic model of abnormal behaviour. (12 marks)

(b) Assess this model in terms of its implications for treatment. (12 marks)   [AEB, June 1998]

Further reading

Graham, H. (1986) *The Human Face Of Psychology*, Milton Keynes: Oxford University Press. (A thorough and readable text which provides good evaluation as well.)

Perls, F., Hefferline, R. and Goodman, P. (1973) *Gestalt Therapy*, Harmondsworth: Penguin. (Conveys the flavour of the original practitioners well.)

Rogers, C. (1961) *On Becoming A Person*, London: Constable. (Readable and persuasive account of Rogers' theorising; worth reading extracts if not the whole text.)

7

Research methods in atypical psychology

General principles of research
Different research methods

General principles of research

Research in the area of atypical psychology is designed to answer a variety of different questions.

- First, it may look at the **prevalence** of different mental disorders by gathering statistics.
- Second, it may explore *attitudes* to mental disorders, using interviews and questionnaires for example.
- Third, the *causes* of mental disorder may be assessed by, for example epidemiological studies, case studies or experimentation.
- Fourth, the *effectiveness* of therapies may be evaluated by outcome studies using a variety of techniques.

To achieve these aims, there is a variety of research methods and techniques available. Although different from one another in many ways, they all have advantages and disadvantages, a similar basis and similar aims. The common basis for all research methods is science, which proceeds by carrying out observations, deriving testable statements ('hypotheses') from those observations, and putting the hypotheses to the test. Ultimately, if hypotheses are upheld when tested, they will be used as the basis for formulating theories which give us an understanding of behaviour as well as the ability to predict and control it. This process is illustrated in Figure 7. 1.

Given that the scientific approach is accepted (and it should be pointed out at this stage that not all psychologists do in fact accept it – humanistic psychologists, for example, regard it as being too mechanistic and insufficiently individualistic to deal with the complexities of human experience), what does this imply for the way in which research is carried out? Three points need to be considered here: objectivity; reliability; validity.

Objectivity

If a study is objective, it should not be biased by the behaviour and expectations of the researcher. This means that it should yield the same results no matter who carries out the study. To achieve this, standardised procedures will need to be used to ensure uniformity of behaviour with all participants. Scales to measure aggression, for example, should yield the same rating for equivalent behaviours in different individuals, and different raters should interpret and use the

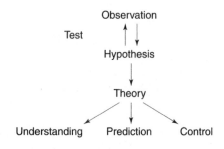

Figure 7.1 **The way that science proceeds**

scale in identical ways. In some cases, it may be necessary to use research assistants who themselves have no idea what the hypothesis of the study is (called a 'double blind' procedure), so that they cannot influence the results in any one particular direction.

Reliability

The requirement for **reliability** goes one step further, to enforce the principle of consistency. Reliability demands that not only should different researchers measure behaviours in the same way, but that different studies carried out at different times, in different places, with different participants, should all yield the same results (provided of course that they are broadly comparable). Similarly, if the same participants are measured repeatedly, they should give comparable results on the different occasions.

Validity

Validity demands that the study really is measuring what it claims to be measuring. This can be looked at from several different viewpoints. Internal validity is assessed by looking at the size of the effect measured – could it be due to chance? Are there any influential factors which have not been taken into account? Early studies of the causes of schizophrenia, for example, showed differences in iodine levels in the body compared to normal individuals. This turned out to be the result of hospital dietary inadequacies, rendering the research invalid.

'External validity' refers to how well the findings generalise from the sample studied to other people, places (known as 'ecological validity') or measures (known as 'concurrent validity'). A particular drug may be effective with one group of schizophrenics, for example, but will it work with all types? Will it be effective in everyday life as well as in a hospital setting? Are the effects general or just restricted to one aspect of behaviour? Do self-report and observational measures yield the same results?

Choice of research method, then, will depend on a consideration of how well each method can fulfil these criteria in a given situation, and also on the practicalities of using particular methods in that given situation. The area under investigation will determine how useful a given method is likely to be, and also how ethical it will be to apply it.

Some methods, for example, can tell us very little about the causes of behaviour, only about how common it is. Other methods can tell us about causes but may be unethical in some situations because they could be harmful to participants, or they may lack ecological validity. In the following section we will look at a range of methods and consider their advantages and disadvantages. The methods we will be covering are: epidemiological research; surveys; case studies; correlational studies; experiments; meta-analyses.

Progress exercise

What is the difference between objectivity, reliability and validity? How can researchers ensure that their studies demonstrate all three?

Different research methods

Epidemiological research

Epidemiological research is the study of the frequency and distribution of illness in a population (Davison and Neale 1990). Large samples of the populace will be studied in order to ascertain the **prevalence** of illness (or disorder) – i.e. the proportion of the population who are sufferers – or the **incidence** – the number of new cases that occur in a given population over a particular period. This research may employ statistical analyses of data from medical practitioners. The obvious disadvantage of using these data is that not all cases may seek treatment. An example of this type of research is a study by Marks (1970) of out-patients seen at the Maudsley Hospital in London, which revealed that 5 per cent of all cases seen had phobic disorders. Of these, 60 per cent had agoraphobia, which has a rate of occurrence of 0.6 per cent in the general population. Another example is the research by Robins *et al.* (1984), in which residents in a given area were sampled and given diagnostic interviews. These were used to estimate the lifetime prevalence of different disorders (the proportion of people who have ever experienced the disorder). The data obtained from 9,000 people are shown in Table 7.1.

Evaluation

Such research can give clues about the causes of disorders as well; if a particular disorder is more common in a particular group of people it is important to ask why that may be. For example, schizophrenia has a higher prevalence in poorer areas. This could either be because some aspect of poverty is a causal factor in schizophrenia, or because schizophrenics move to poorer areas as a result of their disorder and its effects on their finances (social drift hypothesis).

Epidemiological research alone cannot establish the causes of disorder; it can, however, identify *risk factors* which appear to increase the likelihood of the disorder developing. For example, Brown and Harris (1978) in their London study found a higher incidence of depression in working-class housewives than in any other group

Table 7.1 Lifetime prevalence of different disorders (Robins *et al.* 1984)

Disorder	New Haven	Baltimore	St. Louis
Schizophrenia	1.9%	1.6%	1.0%
Major depressive episode	6.7%	3.7%	5.5%
Manic episode	1.1%	0.6%	1.1%
Phobia	7.8%	23.3%	9.4%
Panic disorder	1.4%	1.4%	1.5%
Obsessive-compulsive	2.6%	3.0%	1.9%
Anorexia	0%	0.1%	0.1%
Alcohol abuse/dependence	11.5%	13.7%	15.7%
Antisocial personality	2.1%	2.6%	3.3%

studied. Associated risk factors were short-term life events such as bereavement, together with long-term adversity such as unemployment.

Surveys

These typically involve the use of questionnaires, either sent through the mail or administered in interviews to a large sample of the population. For example, Jones and Cochrane (1981) used questionnaires to ascertain the extent to which laypersons have a stereotype of mental illness, and found clear differences in the ways that 'normal' and 'mentally ill' people were described.

Evaluation

Surveys provide a rapid source of large amounts information that can give a good overview of attitudes, provided they are based on adequate sampling of the population. They can suffer from non-response bias in that those who choose not to respond may represent a particular sector of the populace or a particular type of attitude, for example. They can also be distorted by social desirability responding, which is the tendency of some respondents to give the response that portrays them in a favourable light, rather than saying what they really think. Surveys may not always give a good indication of actual behaviour, as they are based on reports by participants of how they think they behave, or would behave, in given situations. Additionally, they do not explain *why* people think or act as they do.

Correlational studies

This method attempts to make links between variables (a 'variable' is anything that can vary, from attitude, personality and behaviour, to social class). The variables of interest are measured in the sample of participants, and a statistic known as a correlation coefficient is calculated to show the extent to which the variables are related. For example, several studies into the genetic basis of manic-depression (e.g. Allen 1976) have looked at the extent to which twins are concordant for the disorder (concordance is a way of measuring correlation). The finding that identical twins appear to be more

RESEARCH METHODS IN ATYPICAL PSYCHOLOGY

similar than non-identical twins is then used to argue the case that manic-depression has a significant genetic component.

Evaluation

Again, correlation is an indicator of possible causation – nothing more. For example, members of a family who are closely related tend to show quite strong correlations between their behaviour, but this is just as likely to be the result of the fact that they share similar environments as it is to result from shared genes.

Case studies

These are generally long-term, in-depth studies of an individual (or small group of individuals). They include a wealth of biographical material, both past and present, obtained from interviews with the individual concerned, family, friends and colleagues, material from official records and documents (e.g. school, employment, medical), and information obtained from psychometric tests (such as IQ tests) and therapeutic interviews (if appropriate). This approach is described as *idiographic*, because it focuses on one individual – as opposed to the *nomothetic* approach used by most research (such as surveys), with its focus on group behaviour and general laws.

Evaluation

Examples have been given throughout the text of case studies that illustrate the application of the different therapies discussed. Suffice it to say here that the method is very useful for exploring unusual cases (such as the case of multiple personality reported by Thigpen and Cleckley (1954) known as 'The Three Faces Of Eve') and the application of new treatments. In some cases it is in fact the only method available because the disorder is so rare. It allows change over time to be observed and is very wide-ranging in its coverage of possible influences on behaviour, hence it can suggest hypotheses for more precise testing.

However, the case study method also has many disadvantages. Because the cases studied are generally unusual ones, it is often difficult to generalise from them to the rest of the population; generalising from a single case is always a dubious practice anyway, and in this instance it is doubly so because they are far from being representative cases. The degree of involvement of researcher and participant over a long period of time is also a problem, as it is more likely that bias may be introduced into interpretation and recording of what goes on. Freud, you may remember, was accused of this. The method gives no more than an indication of cause and effect; even if a therapy appears to produce change, it could be the result of some other factor of which the researcher is unaware, or recovery may have occurred at that point in time even without the therapeutic intervention. Finally, the ethics of case studies has also given cause for concern. Although confidentiality is provided by the use of pseudonyms in most cases, some writers still feel that the individuals studied have been treated as nothing more than human guinea-pigs.

Experiments and quasi-experiments

The most scientific of all the methods is the experiment. This is because it permits cause and effect to be identified through the manipulation of one variable (called the **independent variable**) and observation of the effects of this on another variable (called the **dependent variable**). Provided that all other variables which may influence the results (known as 'confounding variables') are controlled (i.e. kept at constant levels throughout), then any changes in the dependent variable can be attributed to the manipulation of the independent variable. This is often achieved by having a *control group* whose members are treated identically to the *experimental group* throughout, in all respects but one. For example, Phillips (1963; cited in Orford 1963) explored the effects of psychiatric labelling on social distance (attitudes indicating how closely people would want to interact with the person described) by presenting participants with descriptions of psychiatric cases with or without their psychiatric labels attached. The fact that greater social distance (i.e. less contact) was preferred when labels were attached gave an indication of the prejudice that labels can confer.

Although most experiments are carried out on groups, it is also possible (and particularly useful in clinical research) to carry out experiments on single cases. One way of doing this is to use a **reversal design**, whereby a baseline measurement (control condition) is made of the incidence of problem behaviours, followed by the application of a treatment (experimental condition). The treatment is then withdrawn for a period and then re-applied. If the application of treatment can be seen to be associated with change it is likely that it is a causal influence. Thus Tate and Baroff (1966) showed that self-injury in a psychotic boy (e.g. banging his head against the wall) could be reduced by treatment involving the provision of extra affection, and its withdrawal whenever he attempted to injure himself.

The problem with the above approach is that it is not always possible to reverse the treatment (psychosurgery, for example, cannot be reversed), and even where it is possible to do so, it may not be ethical to allow participants to relapse. Therefore in some cases a **multiple baseline procedure** might be used instead, whereby several behaviours are monitored and treatment applied to one at a time. For example, a self-injuring child who was also unable to sit still might be rewarded for change in one behaviour only at first, then for the other as well (Dallos and Cullen 1990).

Because of the difficulty in generalising from a single case, many researchers prefer to use a **between groups comparison design** (BGCD) where an experimental and a control group are compared after the experimental group is subjected to some sort of treatment. The randomised controlled trial (or clinical trial) is the most effective way of doing this, and involves the random allocation of participants to either an experimental (treatment) or a control group. For example, research into the effects of behaviour therapy may allocate phobics at random to a therapy or a control group (often given a placebo or dummy treatment) in order to evaluate the effectiveness of a course of treatment.

Evaluation

The experimental method is useful to permit the analysis of cause and effect. Statistical analysis of results can provide an objective assessment of the likelihood of the outcome being obtained by chance. A result is generally considered to be statistically significant if there are fewer than five chances in 100 that it is obtained by chance. However, the method does raise issues about ethics, and about validity (both of which will be discussed in detail in Chapter 8). Use of a control group in clinical trials is a particular problem, since people who need treatment are effectively being denied it for the duration of the study.

One alternative is to use **analogue experiments**, where a related problem is studied. For example, rather than study real phobic patients, students with fear of public speaking have been used as an analogue to test the effectiveness of therapies (Paul 1967). Another variation on this is to simulate mental disorder in the laboratory. Administration of a lactate infusion, for example, can bring on the symptoms of a panic attack (see Clark 1992 in Chapter 11). In both cases, the external validity (or 'realism') of the study is sacrificed for the sake of ethics. A final possibility is to use a **quasi-experiment**, which takes advantage of naturally-occurring changes in an independent variable. This is not a true experiment, because the independent variable is not directly manipulated. It does, however, avoid ethical criticisms associated with the direct manipulation of variables. For example, therapies may be compared by looking at the effectiveness of therapists who use two different approaches to therapy. The problem here is that it is not always possible to control all of the other variables in the situation that could influence the outcomes. In the example given, the use of different therapists, as well as the different therapeutic approaches, could have a significant influence on therapeutic outcomes.

There is clearly no ideal way to carry out research on behaviour; this may be more evident when considering atypical behaviour than in any other area of psychology. In practice, mixed designs incorporating elements of several of the methods discussed above may be employed, and theories built on evidence gleaned from a range of research.

Progress exercise

What is meant by the following terms:

1 Reversal design
2 Multiple baseline procedure
3 Between-groups comparison design
4 A randomised controlled trial?

Meta-analysis

This is a recent technique of particular importance in the study of mental disorder. The aim is to strengthen evidence, particularly where studies have produced conflicting findings, by combining the results from several sources. This can be done either by the use of a literature review or, more commonly, by statistical combination and re-analysis of data. An example of this approach is the meta-analytic study by Smith *et al.* (1980) which compared the effectiveness of six different types of therapy by re-analysing the results of 475 studies involving 25,000+ participants. Relative to no therapy, all six were found to be effective in helping with problems, the average improvement being 75 per cent better than in the no-therapy group. (This study is discussed further in Chapter 8.)

Evaluation

Meta-analysis is a useful technique for combining large amounts of data, provided that it has all been obtained from well-controlled studies in the first place. However, decisions about which studies are sufficiently well-controlled to be included could be a source of bias. For example, Wilson and Rachman (1983) accused Smith *et al.* of eliminating too many studies of behaviour therapy from their analysis. As Davison and Neale (1990: 561) conclude 'A continuing challenge, in our view, is the seemingly inescapable role of the investigator's own paradigm in judging the merits of another's meta-analysis'.

Chapter summary

The aims of research into atypical behaviour may be to investigate prevalence, attitudes towards the behaviour, causes, or the effectiveness of treatment. Research needs to follow the scientific principles of hypothesis-testing, objectivity, reliability and validity. Methods available include non-experimental methods such as epidemiological research, surveys, correlational studies and case studies, as well as experimental methods. Experimental methods and quasi-experiments can utilise reversal, multiple baseline and between-groups comparison designs. Non-experimental methods give less control over potential confounding variables, but may have more ecological validity. Experimental methods provide more control, but often at the expense of ecological validity. They have also been subject to ethical criticisms for manipulating participants' behaviour. Meta-analysis can be used to combine information from a large number of studies, but it can only be as good as the studies it chooses to analyse.

Review exercise

Draw up a table that displays each of the methods discussed in the chapter. For each, list the advantages, disadvantages, and examples of studies in separate columns (you can find other examples elsewhere in the book).

Sample essay question

Choose one type of therapy and describe how you might assess its effectiveness. Discuss the reasons behind the decisions you make about the design of the study, its procedures, the selection of participants, analysis of results and ethical considerations. (20 marks)

[NEAB, February 1996]

Further reading

Barkham, M. (1990) 'Research in individual therapy', in W. Dryden (ed.) *Individual Therapy: A Handbook*, Milton Keynes: Oxford University Press. (Gives a good summary of the practical issues.)

Coolican, H. (1994) *Research Methods and Statistics in Psychology*, London: Hodder & Stoughton. (Good coverage of methodology, together with useful evaluation.)

8

Evaluation of therapy

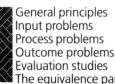
General principles

In practical terms, 'research is often invoked as a method of establishing whether or not to provide a service, or which service to provide' (Parry 1996). In other words, we need research to tell us which treatments are effective. This, however, is only part of the picture; we also need to know which types of behaviour a treatment is effective for, in which types of people, and which aspects of the therapeutic process are effective. In other words, research needs to look at input, outcome and process (Orlinsky and Howard 1987).

The *input* phase consists of all of those elements which are brought to the therapy session, including the characteristics of the client and the therapist. The *process* phase deals with what takes place during the session – for example, the development of a relationship between the therapist and client, the interventions made by the therapist and the insights achieved by the client. The *outcome* is assessed with reference to the changes occurring in the client, both long- and short-term, that can be attributed to the therapy.

Any attempt at evaluation of therapy may focus on one or several of these aspects; this is equally evident whether the evaluation is based on a single therapy or whether it attempts to compare different therapies. When examining research in this area, it is important to identify which aspect(s) of input, process and outcome each study is concerned with.

As discussed in Chapter 7, the initial choice of research method has implications for the quality of the research, for its reliability and validity, and for its ability to demonstrate causal links between variables. There are a great many other problems associated with the evaluation of research in this area, however, and in this chapter we will begin by discussing what these problems are, before we move on to look at samples of studies which aim to evaluate the therapies themselves.

Input problems

At the input end of the research, there are four problems to consider.

1 *Adequacy of the classification system* used is the first of these. It has already been pointed out in Chapter 1 that the system in use at the moment (namely, DSM IV) is not totally reliable, and that some categories (e.g. schizophrenia) appear to contain individuals who display widely differing behaviours. If research is carried out on participants whose diagnosis is uncertain (which is certainly the case with some of the early studies) then it will not be very enlightening. For example, Crow *et al.* (1982) have suggested that Type I symptoms of schizophrenia (such as hallucinations and delusions) may be treatable by drugs, but Type II symptoms such as loss of emotional responsiveness and social withdrawal are not. Thus the type of schizophrenic symptoms exhibited by the research sample could be crucial in determining the outcome of treatment. An allied point relates to the use of analogue groups (see previous chapter) in clinical research. Where studies have employed students with fear of public speaking rather than real phobic patients, for example, it has to be established that their findings are equally relevant to clients with diagnosed phobias.

2 *Current medication* is the second problem. Where this is not the treatment being evaluated, it could easily confound the results. Early studies of cognitive functioning in schizophrenia, for example, reported attentional problems that could equally well have resulted from the medication being taken as from the disorder itself. Some types of medication may have more side effects than others, and some therapies may be more affected by medication than others. Hence it is advisable for all participants to have been withdrawn from medication for some time before the study is carried out in order to ensure that results are attributable to the procedures under investigation.

3 *Random sampling* is the third problem. For experiments in particular, it is important that participants are allocated to conditions randomly in order for the study to be valid. If either the control or the treatment group contains the less severe cases, for example, the results will not give an accurate reflection of the usefulness of the treatment. For ethical reasons, random allocation can only be done with the consent of the patient/participant and their GP. In practice, GPs may be unwilling to do this; the treatment group has as a consequence been found to be often younger and less severely ill (Parry 1996).

Patient consent is also a difficult issue, as it could be argued that people who suffer from mental disorder are not always able to appreciate fully what it is that they are consenting to. They may refuse to join a clinical trial, making the sample non-random because their characteristics may differ in important ways from those who do participate. Or, if they have a preference for a particular option and do not get offered it, they may drop out of the study, again creating bias in the sample. This is particularly likely with drug trials, where according to Parry (1996: 284), 'therapy and drug comparisons mask a very high attrition rate in the patients recruited to the drug treatment group, and many people seem to find therapy more acceptable than drugs'. This also raises the question of how well results transfer into real-life settings, where patients are not randomly assigned and their preferences are taken into account.

4 *Therapist characteristics* is the final problem. Research has often demonstrated that the originator of a therapeutic approach appears to have more success with using it than do subsequent users, indicating that skill, enthusiasm or even personal charisma may be important. Research is likely to involve practitioners who subscribe to and are skilled in the use of a particular therapy; this is less likely to be

the case in real-life practice, where a practitioner may need to be multi-skilled and may have no particular enthusiasm for any one therapy.

Process problems

When process is considered, there are two levels on which issues can be raised. If the therapeutic process is being considered as a whole, the question to be asked is: 'What is being compared with what?' In a **reversal design**, a baseline is established, and individuals can then be compared with themselves. In a **between groups comparison**, a control group will be used, and it is the nature of this control group that is controversial.

Typically, a **placebo**, or inert treatment will be given to the control group to provide a baseline measure against which the effects of treatment can be compared. This can vary from being put on a waiting list, or given inert tablets instead of active drugs, to being allowed to see a counsellor. Clearly, these would have very different consequences. Many studies have employed placebo conditions that cannot legitimately be described as inert substitutes for treatment. Waiting lists and counselling, for example, provide different levels of support. Kirsch and Sapirstein (1998) have pointed out that in clinical drug trials, people who experience side effects will be alerted to the fact that they have been given the active drug and not the placebo. Thus their expectations may be different to those of the placebo group, and they may show a greater response to treatment for this reason. What is needed are 'active placebos' which are able to mimic the side effects of the drug but have no therapeutic effects.

Other studies have attempted to compare the effects of two different types of therapy, such as psychoanalysis and behavioural treatments. This approach too can encounter problems, since the aims, target populations and time scales of the two procedures are often not comparable. Psychoanalysis, for example, is a slow procedure which may not be effective over the time available for the study, but may be useful in the long term. Behavioural treatment is very rapid in most cases, but the effects may not necessarily be long-lasting.

Studies of the type mentioned above have often shown that there is little to choose between the effectiveness of different therapeutic approaches, which has led some researchers to argue that the focus of research needs to be shifted to investigate the basic principles of change common to all therapies. This leads us into a consideration of the second kind of issue that needs to be dealt with here, which is the attempt to separate different components of therapy and ascertain which is the most effective. This can be done across the range of therapies, as outlined earlier, or within one type of therapy. For example, systematic desensitisation could be investigated to see if relaxation or graduated exposure appeared to be the most important feature in successful outcomes. The problem that this raises is, first, whether components can be separated in this way, and second, whether they can in fact be manipulated. For example, it is difficult to see how unconditional positive regard could be achieved without empathy in Rogerian therapy; it would also be difficult to prevent transference in psychoanalysis.

Outcome problems

It is when it comes to outcome that researchers face their biggest problems. The first issue here is the definition of cure. Given the different models of mental disorder that exist, it is hardly surprising that practitioners of different therapies view the outcome in very different ways. Those subscribing to the behavioural model look for the disappearance of symptoms, for example, whereas humanistic and existential therapists do not accept that 'cure' is a relevant concept. For example, when asked if Kingsley Hall was a success, one resident replied: 'That is an irrelevant question: it does no harm, it does no "cure" ' (Barnes and Berke 1982: 371). Even within a perspective, such as the medical model, it is possible to regard the suppression of symptoms by drugs rather differently to their elimination by psychosurgery.

One possible answer is to look for *change* rather than *cure*, but change is not easily measured either. It may be quantitative (such as change in the amount of anxiety displayed when a spider is encountered) or qualitative, whereby the type of behaviour displayed changes (for example, aggressive responses may be replaced by assertive responses). There is also the possibility of change being negative; we will come back to this later. The significance of the change is typically assessed statistically in terms of how likely it is that a change of the magnitude observed would have occurred through chance alone. A statistically significant change, however, need not necessarily be clinically significant if it does not lead to an improved quality of life for the client. Detectable physiological changes in anxiety may not, for instance, be associated with overt behavioural change, or with sufficient change to bring behaviour within the 'normal' range.

Then there is the difficulty posed by the possibility of **spontaneous remission** (Eysenck 1952). This is the fact that many disorders disappear of their own accord in the course of time. Spontaneous remission rates can be calculated, and have been estimated by Eysenck to be as high as 66 per cent. Bergin and Lambert (1978), however, estimated that a figure of 30–60 per cent of patients is more realistic, the rate of spontaneous remission varying according to the type of disorder. Malan *et al.* (1975) noted that in many studies untreated individuals have an assessment interview at least, which could be sufficient to influence them to change. Thus the recovery observed is not truly spontaneous, even though it does occur without psychotherapy. Whatever the percentage of patients affected, and whatever the explanation for the phenomenon, clearly any estimate of the effectiveness of therapy must take it into account; this is one reason for having control conditions.

Another phenomenon, which has been called the **hello-goodbye effect**, could also confound results. This refers to the observation that at the start of therapy ('hello') clients may exaggerate their symptoms in order to get attention. At the end ('goodbye'), on the other hand, they may minimise their problems in order to make the therapy seem worthwhile. This could obviously affect estimates of the amount of change produced.

Finally, it is necessary to consider the *time period* for which participants are followed up after treatment. It is essential to carry out such long-term evaluation, but for how long? Six months? A year? Many treatments which yield relatively poor short-term effects may turn out to be cost-effective if they maintain their effectiveness over a longer period. Included in this is the importance of looking for **symptom substitution**, which many psychodynamic therapists argue will result from short-term superficial therapies such as behavioural approaches.

For all of these reasons, reports of evaluation studies must be read very carefully in order to ascertain their utility. In the next section, we will examine some of the better-known examples.

Draw up a table to show the major input, output and process problems in evaluating psychotherapy.

Evaluation studies

These can be divided into two groups, according to whether they are investigating effectiveness of therapists, or the effectiveness of different types of therapy with different types of disorder.

Effectiveness of therapists

Karasu *et al.* (1979) found that matching clients and therapists of similar ages resulted in more productive therapy. Beutler *et al.* (1986) found female therapists to be more effective than males. This latter study also showed that therapist expectations and potential for social influence (in terms of expertise, trustworthiness and attractiveness) affected outcomes.

Ethnic and cultural differences between client and therapist may also be important. Grant (1994) reported that black clients find it difficult to trust a white therapist (and difficult to find a black one!).

Truax and Carkhuff (1964) reported that the most effective therapists are those who try to establish empathic relationships with clients based on genuine caring, trust and respect; without such qualities, the client may show deterioration instead of improvement. This relationship, with its emphasis on warmth and understanding, has been termed the **therapeutic alliance** (Luborsky 1984), and it seems to be a crucial component of all effective therapies.

Effectiveness of different types of therapy related to different disorders

Information relevant to this issue has been given throughout Chapters 2–6, when individual therapies were discussed. What follows is a summary of some of the major studies only.

Looking first at studies indicating the utility of chemotherapy, May (1975) compared drugs, psychoanalysis, drugs plus psychoanalysis, psychoanalytic-type psychotherapy, ECT and milieu therapy among schizophrenics. Rated behaviour and release rates showed that drugs and psychoanalysis plus drugs were the most effective procedures. There was little difference between the two conditions, indicating the predominance of the drugs in producing the observed effects. Another study by Elkins *et al.* (1989) compared cognitive-behavioural therapy, psychodynamic therapy and the antidepressant imipramine as treatments for depression. All treatments were found to be equally effective, except that imipramine was superior in the more severe cases. A study of panic disorders by Klosko *et al.* (1990) found no significant difference in response to treatment by behaviour therapy and the anxiolytic drug aprazolam. A recent study by Piccinelli *et al.* (1995) found that chemotherapy using SSRIs was far superior to a placebo for the short-term treatment of obsessive-compulsive disorder. Grouped together, these studies suggest that drugs are most useful with schizophrenia and severe depression, with possible application to obsessive-compulsive disorder.

Behavioural treatments

These have been researched by Marks and O'Sullivan (1988) in a paper summarised in Chapter 11 of this book. They reviewed studies comparing the effectiveness of drugs and psychological treatments for agoraphobia and obsessive-compulsive disorder, and concluded that neither drugs nor psychological treatments other than exposure therapy were helpful in the long term. Berman and Norton (1985) confirmed that behavioural treatments are more effective with agoraphobia than any other approaches. Cognitive-behavioural therapies have been researched in connection with depression by Miller and Berman (1983), who found that cognitive therapy was slightly more effective with depression than with anxiety disorders, but the differences were not significant. Durham *et al.* (1994) compared cognitive therapy, psychoanalytic therapy and anxiety management training for effectiveness with generalised anxiety disorder. Cognitive therapy was the most effective in producing symptom change, and psychoanalytic therapy the least effective. Clark (1993) reported that cognitive therapy is successful in 90 per cent of cases of panic disorder, compared with 50 per cent of cases cured by chemotherapy. Psychodynamic therapies are more effective with anxiety disorders than they are with schizophrenia (Smith *et al.* 1980), and generally work better with articulate, well-educated and well-motivated individuals – the YAVIS effect.

Studies comparing effectiveness

Clearly, then, there is a pattern emerging which appears to match certain disorders with certain therapies and treatments, although there are some discrepancies. However, in many studies the therapy is simply compared with a placebo condition or its effectiveness compared with two different types of disorder. What we need to know is quite different; we need to know whether a given therapy is better than any other therapy for a particular disorder. Relatively few studies have attempted to do this, and these are mostly meta-analyses. Four are described here.

1   The first study is by Sloane *et al.* (1975), who compared behaviour therapy, psychoanalytically-oriented psychotherapy and no therapy (waiting-list control) in terms of their effectiveness for ninety clients suffering from anxiety and personality disorder. After four months, 80 per cent of the treatment groups had improved, compared with only 48 per cent of the controls. Therefore both types of therapy were considered equally effective and superior to no treatment at all. This study was, however, criticised for the nature of the control group and the fact that the psychotherapy was so brief that it could not do psychoanalytic procedures justice.

2   Smith *et al.* (1980) carried out a meta-analysis of 475 studies, comparing the effectiveness of six different therapies: client-centred; gestalt; behaviour modification; psychodynamic; cognitive-behavioural; and systematic desensitisation. Overall, it was concluded that the improvement in the therapy groups was greater than that of 80 per cent of the control group, but the differences between the therapy groups were not significant.

3   A meta-analysis of nineteen studies by Svartberg and Stiles (1991) found that brief psychodynamic therapy was inferior to alternatives for most disorders, except for mixed neurotic patients. As the follow-up period increased, its inferiority became more noticeable. Cognitive behaviour therapy was especially effective for severe depression.

4   The last study, by Shapiro (1990), comes closest to providing the necessary type of analysis. Shapiro looked at two large meta-analytic studies by Smith *et al.* (1980), who examined 475 studies, and Shapiro and Shapiro (1982). This permitted three therapies – behavioural, cognitive, and psychodynamic/humanistic – and three disorders – neurotic, phobic and emotional/somatic – to be evaluated. The conclusion was that, apart from the inferiority of psychodynamic/humanistic approaches, no clear pattern of effectiveness could be observed.

One possible reason for this might be the large individual differences between the response of clients, even when they are suffering from the same disorder. Cultural factors, for example, have been shown to be associated with significant differences. A meta-analysis by Wittman and Matt (1986) of the effects of psychotherapy in Germany found that the effects in general were only half the size of those reported by Smith *et al.* (1980). Linn *et al.* (1990) have shown that Asian schizophrenics require a smaller dose of neuroleptic drugs than do American schizophrenics for optimal treatment. Sue (1990) found that Asians prefer directive therapies such as behaviour therapy, while Americans prefer non-directive approaches such as Rogerian therapy. Another possible explanation for the similarity in response to different therapies is considered in the next section.

Progress exercise

Decide which treatments would be the most suitable for each of the following disorders, and give evidence to support your choices: phobia; schizophrenia; obsessive-compulsive disorder; anxiety; personality disorder; depression; panic disorder.

The equivalence paradox and negative outcomes

Equivalence paradox

Although there are some differences between therapies, it is clear that in many studies the differences are small. This has been termed the **equivalence paradox** (Stiles *et al*. 1986), and suggests that in many cases it is not the specific processes or techniques of the therapy used that are effective but, rather, more general characteristics to do with the nature of the therapeutic relationship. To quote one commentator:

> it is in fact extremely difficult to escape the conclusion that the most potent aspect of psychotherapy is the solidarity afforded patients through their relationship with someone taking an intense, on-going interest in their welfare. Having someone on one's side makes a genuine, material difference to one's ability to do battle with the world.
>
> (Smail 1996: 92)

Negative outcomes

There is another side to this story. Several studies have indeed demonstrated that psychological treatment is generally superior to no treatment at all, or to a placebo (e.g. Roth and Fonagy 1996; Sloane *et al*. 1975), although even a placebo is effective to some extent (Smith *et al*. 1980). Shapiro and Shapiro (1982) conclude that after therapy the average treated client is better than 80–85 per cent of untreated (control) clients.

However, not all researchers would subscribe to this view. For example, Prioleau *et al*. (1983) argue that only thirty-two out of the 475 studies looked at by Smith *et al*. (1980) were methodologically sound. Re-analysis of data derived from only these sound studies led them to conclude that the benefits of psychotherapy had not been convincingly demonstrated. This conclusion is remarkably similar to that reached by Eysenck (1952) in his much-criticised study of the effectiveness of psychotherapy (psychoanalytic and eclectic). His conclusion was that the data 'fail to prove that psychotherapy, Freudian or otherwise, facilitates the recovery of neurotic patients', and that 'the research should make us seriously question the justification of giving an important place in the training of clinical psychologists to a skill whose existence and effectiveness is still unsupported by any scientifically acceptable evidence' (cited in Gross 1994: 375). Even more worrying is the point made by Smith *et al.* (1980) that some patients do not improve, and around 9 per cent actually get worse after therapy. This figure is almost identical to the figure of 10 per cent quoted by Lambert *et al.* (1986). The debate has been taken even further by Mair (1997) in an analysis of treatment outcomes for fourteen patients suffering from **dissociative identity disorder** (DID), the details of which are given in Case study 8.1. Her conclusion was that not only was the treatment not cost-effective, in that patients were referred to mental health services more frequently after treatment than before, but that there were serious ethical questions to be asked about the consequences of treatment for the patients. They showed an increased incidence of self-harm, suicide attempts and other effects attributable to the recovery of disturbing memories during therapy.

Case study 8.1: Psychological treatment for DID – the risks and benefits (Mair 1997)

The records of a psychiatric hospital were searched for DID patients treated in the period 1988–95, yielding a sample of fourteen female patients aged between twenty-eight and forty-two. They had been treated for an average of three and a half years, reporting two to twenty-one personalities each (an average of nine). Approximately three years after treatment, thirteen of these patients were traced through their GPs to obtain information about their current status.

It was found that after treatment they consulted their GPs slightly more than before. The five whom GPs assessed as having benefited from treatment had tended to drop out of treatment earlier, showed less stress and fewer personalities. The eight patients who showed no benefit or had deteriorated after treatment had had more treatment sessions and showed more personalities. Prior to treatment there were no differences between the two groups.

Thus better outcomes were associated with less treatment. Many patients had recovered memories of severe child abuse that had not been present before treatment, and in some cases this had led to the breakdown of family relationships.

As Eysenck said in 1952 'there appears to be an inverse correlation between recovery and psychotherapy; the more psychotherapy, the smaller the recovery rate' (cited in Gross 1994: 374).

The evaluation presented above is based on scientific approaches to determining the effectiveness of therapy. There is, however, another viewpoint to consider, which is best represented by another quote from Smail (1987: 92):

The alternative to reliance on a technology of change is the cultivation of a society which takes care of its members. A therapy industry cannot replace or take over the function of an ethics of human conduct.

This is the concern of the next chapter.

Chapter summary

The scientific evaluation of therapy raises a variety of problems that need to be considered at the input, process and outcome stages of research. Evaluation studies dealing with the effectiveness of different therapists show that the therapeutic alliance is a crucial component of successful therapy. Studies comparing the effectiveness of different types of therapy show that, for most patients, therapy is more beneficial than no therapy. The most effective therapy will depend on the type of disorder as well as other characteristics of the individual, such as ethnicity. The equivalence paradox refers to the fact that the difference between the effectiveness of various therapies is often small. Success may therefore depend primarily on the provision of a caring relationship. However. therapy may not always be beneficial, and some people appear to deteriorate rather than improve.

Review exercise

Draw up a table to show which type of therapy is the most suitable for treating different types of mental disorder, using the information presented in this and earlier chapters.

Sample essay questions

1. (a) Describe one type of therapy or treatment for mental illness or behavioural disorder. (12 marks)

   (b) Discuss the difficulties of evaluating this type of therapy or treatment. (12 marks)   [AEB, June 1992]

2. Discuss two types of treatment/therapy for abnormal behaviour, including reference to research studies of their effectiveness. (24 marks)   [AEB, June 1996]

Further reading

Eysenck, H. (1952) *The Effects of Psychotherapy: An Evaluation*, in R. Gross *Key Studies in psychology*, London: Hodder & Stoughton, 1994. (Worth reading to find out exactly what was written; useful evaluation provided alongside the original paper.)

Parry, G. (1996) 'Using research to change practice', in T. Heller *et al.* (ed.) *Mental Health Matters*, London: Macmillan. (Thought-provoking critique of the research process and its application to practice.)

9

Ethical issues

General principles

It is important to clarify at the outset what we mean by 'ethics'. The definition which follows is taken from Bloch and Chodoff (1981: 8):

> The study of human conduct with respect to the rightness and wrongness of actions and the goodness and badness of the consequences of those actions.

The treatment of individuals suffering from mental disorder raises some particularly difficult ethical problems, and it is these that we will be considering in this chapter.

The Mental Health Act and its implications

The legal position as regards compulsory hospitalisation and treatment in England and Wales is defined by the 1983 Mental Health Act. Compulsory hospitalisation is most likely to be applied when the individuals concerned are felt to be a health and safety risk to themselves (e.g. are suicidal) or to others (e.g. are violent). The Act contains several different sections (hence the term 'sectioning'), details of which are given in Table 9.1.

Commitment can be carried out using a place of safety, restraint of voluntary patient, emergency assessment or assessment order, as

Table 9.1 The main sections of the Mental Health Act (1983)

Type of detention	How long it lasts	Who can arrange it	Medical recommendation needed
Place of safety	Maximum 3 days	Policeman	None
Restraint of voluntary patient	Maximum 3 days	Doctor in charge	Doctor's report
Emergency assessment	Maximum 3 days	Nearest relative or approved social worker	One doctor (patient's own if possible)
Assessment	Maximum 28 days	Nearest relative or approved social worker	Two doctors (1 approved specialist, 1 acquainted with patient, only 1 on hospital staff)
Treatment	Maximum 6 months renewable for 6 months, then 1-year periods	Nearest relative or approved social worker	Two doctors (1 approved specialist, 1 acquainted with patient, only 1 on hospital staff)
Guardianship	Maximum 6 months renewable for 6 months, then one-year periods	Nearest relative or approved social worker	Two doctors (1 approved specialist, 1 acquainted with patient, only 1 on hospital staff)

described above. A guardianship order puts the individual in the care of a responsible person, such as a relative. In practice, the principle of the **Least Restrictive Alternative** will be used when deciding which section to apply. This states that the least restrictive alternative to freedom is to be provided, and confinement should only be applied when no other accommodation is available.

Treatment requires a treatment order, and if it is not an emergency the patient's consent is still required before it can be administered. In practice, this means that only the short-term use of drugs can be permitted without consent. Long-term drug treatment, ECT, psychosurgery or hormone treatment all require consent, as they are not emergency treatments.

Problems arise when the patient can be considered incapable of giving informed consent, as in the case of schizophrenic patients and those suffering from mental retardation, for example. In such cases, non-emergency treatment has been given without the patient's consent in the past. The finding of Devine and Fernald (1973) that patients do better if given a choice about their treatment suggests that this practice is neither practically nor ethically sound. Case study 9.1 provides a basis for arguing that such practices may no longer be permissible, and this ruling has subsequently been extended to any form of invasive treatment. However, the client's health, life and well-being, and the opinions of other professionals will also be important determinants of decisions reached in such cases.

Case study 9.1: Treating sectioned patients without consent

A High Court ruling gave the go-ahead for a 35 year-old woman with a mental age of 5 to be sterilised to prevent unwanted pregnancies. The patient's mother had applied for the order, but at the court of appeal Lord Donaldson ruled that non-emergency medical treatment given to adult mental patients (i.e. those over the age of 18 years) incapable of giving their consent was not legal.

(Guardian 17 January 1989)

Most hospital admissions and treatments for mental disorder are voluntary in practice, only 7 per cent of patients being officially recorded as compulsorily detained under sections of the Mental Health Act. However, it has been argued that many 'voluntary' admissions are in fact coerced. Rogers (1993) looked at the reports of 412 voluntary patients and found that 44 per cent of these were pressurised into entering hospital voluntarily under threat of forced admission. Most of these were young, single schizophrenics.

Consequences extend beyond the loss of individual liberty and the possibility of compulsory treatment. There are many opportunities for abuse; for example, the detention of political dissidents in mental hospitals in Soviet Russia. Sectioned individuals also lose other rights such as gun licences, and voting rights, and they are disqualified from jury service. Divorce is no longer obtainable on the grounds of admission to mental hospital, but can be obtained eventually on the basis of desertion. The mail of a detained person (both incoming and outgoing) can be intercepted if it is felt likely to be distressing or detrimental to treatment. The only exception to this is if the patient is writing to a mental health review tribunal, the Home Secretary, or to any other person or body with the power to order the patient's discharge. Even short admissions carry the risk of patients losing their homes (Bean and Mounser 1993) or their jobs. Outpatient treatment may also threaten employment and social support.

It has been pointed out (Szasz 1962) that compulsory admission cannot be enforced for physical illness. Therefore, if the medical model is followed and mental disorder is seen as an illness with a physiological basis, such powers of detention are inappropriate. Not only are the patient's rights lost, there is the issue of stigmatisation to consider; a psychiatric history will, for example, make it more difficult for an individual to find employment in the future.

Another problem is the possibility of **institutionalisation** (Goffman 1961), whereby long-stay patients may become incapable of supporting themselves in the real world, because they have become dependent on the institution or because society has changed so much since they were a part of it. Mistreatment by staff cannot be disregarded (Martin 1985) as evidenced by the recent reports about special hospitals such as Ashworth and Rampton. An important principle noted by Eastman (1996) in his suggestions for reform is that of reciprocity; given that civil liberties are being infringed by such detention, it is essential that detention is accompanied by adequate treatment rather than the limited treatment currently available in the National Health System.

Implications for criminal law

Another aspect of the Mental Health Act is, of course, its application to criminal cases, where it can affect proceedings in two main ways: first, judgements about whether the individual is competent to stand trial; second, judgements about whether the individual was sane at the time of the crime (the insanity defence). Space precludes detailed consideration of the issues involved here, but clearly such pleas can significantly affect the outcomes for the individuals concerned.

Name three 'sections' of the Mental Health Act. See if you can remember, for each one, who can arrange detention and how long it lasts.

Progress exercise

Ethical issues in diagnosis

The first stage in the 'career' of a mentally disordered individual is likely to be diagnosis. Since this lays the groundwork for what follows, it clearly has ethical implications. The effects of misdiagnosis are considerable, as discussed above, ranging from loss of freedom and compulsory noxious treatment to life-long labelling and legal and social disadvantage.

Misdiagnosis – that is, the inappropriate application of diagnostic categories – is divided by Reich (1981) into two types: purposeful and non-purposeful.

Purposeful misdiagnosis

This could occur through the application of pressure by the individual's family (either through concern for the person's welfare or because they want a troublesome individual removed and dealt with elsewhere), or by the state (which may want political dissidents, for example, to be dealt with in what appears to be a humane way). Pressure may also be brought to bear by the individual concerned. A criminal wanting to avoid being brought to trial and made to face the consequences of a crime may apply for a psychiatric diagnosis, or a woman wanting an abortion may seek such categorisation in order to provide medical justification. In all of the above cases, the aim is other than psychiatric, and there is an awareness in some parties that the label is inappropriate. They share the consequences, however, that harm will be done to either the individual concerned or to the integrity of the clinician (or both).

Non-purposeful misdiagnosis

This is more subtle, and constitutes the greater part of the problem. It can be seen to derive from three sources. First, some misdiagnosis will result from the subjectivity of the criteria used for classification, and the unreliability that is inherent in the system itself. Second, the cultural models and assumptions about mental disorder may create difficulties. Some cultures would not tend to put individuals forward for diagnosis in the first place because the community deals with the behaviours itself and does not regard them as a problem. As mentioned in Chapter 1, in many parts of Nigeria only 40 per cent of the populace considers a description of a paranoid schizophrenic to represent someone who is mentally ill, compared with 90–100 per cent of Americans who do (Erinosho and Ayonrinde 1981).

The assumptions of clinicians have also been examined. Cochrane and Sashidharan (1995) report that it is assumed that the norms for behaviour are those of the white majority, and any departure from these is regarded as pathological. The diagnostic system itself was devised with white norms in mind. The effects of this can be seen in the tendency to overdiagnose schizophrenia in West Indian and Asian immigrants to the UK (Cochrane 1977).

Third, diagnoses can also be applied inappropriately when they provide reassurance that the disturbed behaviour is a recognised medical problem that will respond to treatment, and can be used to relieve the individual of responsibility, as in criminal cases. (An example of this is the case of Beverley Allitt, a nurse who was accused of murdering several babies of whom she was in charge, and who was subsequently diagnosed as suffering from Munchhausen's disease by proxy, a desire to harm those she cares for.) On the other hand, they can be used negatively, to violate the freedom of individuals and exclude them from society, amounting to a form of punishment.

Clearly, then, this is an ethical as well as a practical issue, and has a great many implications for what follows, as this quote makes clear:

> The doctor–patient relationship, as with any other helper–helpee interaction, often turns out to be the most unhelpful of all kinds of human relationships. Once it becomes the doctor's responsibility to solve a patient's problems, the patient can comfortably keep them. It is not his fault if they do not get solved, it is the doctor's.
>
> (Malleson 1973: 97)

Ethical issues in treatment

Choice of treatment

The relationship between diagnosis and treatment is often poor, so that the same presenting problem may be treated differently depending on the facilities and specialists available, and on the clinician's preferences. To some extent, individual differences in case history, causation circumstances and temperament may justify this, but other cases may be decided on pragmatic grounds rather than scientific ones (going back to Eastman's (1996) point about appropriate services not always being available). This is an ethical issue insofar as the consequences for the client of inappropriate treatment may be considerable.

Duration of treatment

This may also be determined by cost rather than by patient needs (e.g. it may be too short in the NHS and too long in private practice). Treatments which are rapid-acting may be offered in preference to more long-term approaches, even if their effectiveness is short-lived.

Effectiveness of treatment

The extent to which treatments have been adequately evaluated for the disorder concerned can also be queried, and such evaluation could be regarded as an ethical necessity, given the potential for harm (Mair 1997). The probability of success should be assessed (if in fact it is known) and discussed with the patient.

Goals of treatment

It has been argued that many therapies are aimed at inducing conformity in the client. Aversion therapy, for example, has been used in the past with homosexuals to help them achieve a 'normal' sexual orientation. Currently, there is greater emphasis than before on respecting the client's individuality while helping them to achieve a more realistic adaptation to society and to cope better with their difficulties. Whether goal-setting is a joint enterprise or not, however, the orientation of the therapist could have a significant effect on the way that the client approaches therapy. The differing needs of the client, the client's family, and society in general can be a source of major conflict for both client and therapist. The ethical need to ensure that the rights of all parties are taken into consideration may be particularly problematic when family therapy is being undertaken, for example.

Type of treatment

Individual therapeutic approaches also have their own particular ethical problems to face. *Behavioural techniques*, for example, have been criticised in the past for being manipulative. The use of food deprivation, 'time out' (which can extend to isolation), and aversive procedures as reinforcement have all been criticised as violations of human rights. A recent example of this is the 'pin down' system operated by some social services units for disturbed adolescents, where solitary confinement and Complan (milk-based meal substitute) were employed to eliminate undesirable behaviour, resulting in public outcry. Aversive procedures have been toned down in recent years, as the 'Smell, Swish and Spit' system discussed in Chapter 4 demonstrates. Exposure therapies such as flooding may also be harmful, leading to increased blood pressure and even heart attacks if not used carefully.

Modern behaviour therapists go to some lengths to include clients in the setting of goals and often put the client in charge of administering reinforcement (then known as 'self-reinforcement) as well. When working with clients who are unable to relate or to understand the problems, such as extreme psychotics or the severely mentally impaired, the issue of participation in decision-making becomes a very real one. This type of therapy is still criticised by many for dehumanising the client, by seeing the symptoms which need treatment as separate from the rest of the person. The fact that any underlying problem is not being treated and could cause difficulties at a later stage is also an ethical dilemma.

Somatic therapies pose a different set of ethical issues, primarily as a result of the side effects associated with their use (described in detail in Chapter 2). For example, the sedation produced by minor tranquillisers can lead to an increased risk of domestic and driving accidents. Major tranquillisers can cause permanent physical damage such as tardive dyskinesia, and lithium can cause kidney damage. Because so many of these treatments have associated side effects, it is often the case that a **cost-benefit analysis** has to be carried out to determine if the benefits will outweigh the costs. This in itself is no easy task when our knowledge about the method of operation of many treatments, such as ECT and the antimanic drugs, is still incomplete. Such decisions should be discussed with the patient wherever possible, although there will be some cases where the patient may not be capable of understanding the issues. This in itself may be difficult to ascertain with any degree of certainty. For example Irwin *et al.* (1985) found that only 25 per cent of patients who claimed to understand the costs and benefits of treatment really had an understanding when questioned closely. The patient should be informed of any hazards and his/her 'informed consent' to the treatment should be obtained. The use of drugs as a substitute for treatment (as 'chemical strait-jackets'), or as an easy solution to stress and sub-clinical depression could also be criticised. Illich (1975) has referred to the 'medicalisation of life', meaning that we have come to expect that we will be given prescriptions to help us to cope. As Malleson (1973: 77) notes: 'For only 15% of 300 consecutive patients seen by me in a London general practice was it acceptable for me to prescribe a drug. However…to lower my prescribing rate as much as this...would have caused a waiting-room rebellion'.

The major issue with *psychoanalysis* has always been that of control by the therapist; the power balance lies very much with the therapist, and abuse is easy (Masson 1988). An egalitarian relationship is advocated instead, but many (e.g. Parsons 1951) feel that this may shake the patient's confidence in the treatment. Reliance on professionals may be a dubious trait to cultivate, but whether the start of therapy is the best time and place to attempt to dislodge it is a matter for careful consideration. Along with other insight therapies, there are also concerns about the emotional distress aroused during therapy. This was noted by Mair (1997) with reference to recovered memories (real or false) about child abuse (see Chapter 8).

Progress exercise

Draw up a table to show the ethical problems raised by each different type of therapy.

Sexual abuse

Another aspect of the therapist–client relationship that has caused concern, regardless of the type of therapy under consideration, is the issue of sexual abuse. A survey of ethical dilemmas encountered by members of the British Psychological Society (Lindsay and Colley 1995) identified 6 per cent of reported dilemmas as relating to sexual issues. Some of these were staff–student relationships, others were therapist–client and therapist–ex-client. Garrett (1994) reported from a review of studies that 10 per cent of therapists admit to sexual contact with one or more clients. Many individual practitioners, however, have admitted to multiple abuse; in one study this accounted for 80% of the clinical psychologists who participated. Legally, this only constitutes a problem if force or fraud are involved, but since such encounters represent an abuse of power and have negative thera-peutic effects, they still pose an ethical question.

Sexism

Some writers (e.g. Worell and Remer 1992) have argued that the classification system for mental disorder is biased, and that females showing standard female behaviour will be more likely to be placed into certain categories (such as histrionic personality disorder, as shown by Hamilton *et al*. 1986). In therapy, too, it is possible to see dependency as the norm for females but not for males. The stereo-types of the therapist could therefore encourage different behaviours. Treatment could also be biased in other ways. For example, some ther-apeutic approaches view schizophrenia or infantile autism as the consequences of living with a pathological mother: consequently, the therapist may be more disposed to view the mother of the family in this way rather than any other family member, or may ignore other potential causes of the problem.

Cultural issues

As discussed in Chapter 8, members of different cultural groups may respond differently to different types of treatment and to different therapists. This needs to be taken into account when arriving at a culturally sensitive decision about what will be appropriate for a particular individual (Baron 1989). There are also cultural biases in choice of treatment. Fernando (1988), for example, has reported that West Indians are most likely to be compulsorily admitted, West Indian, Indian and African patients are more likely to be put on locked wards, and Asians are more likely to receive ECT.

Confidentiality

It is possible that the therapist may be under pressure to divulge infor-mation about a client in some circumstances. This is a legal requirement if the case involves child abuse, or if the client is under investigation in connection with the Prevention of Terrorism Act (1989). Otherwise, according to the Police and Criminal Evidence Act (1984), access to records requires a search warrant signed by a judge.

This may be done for legal reasons, the therapist being instructed by a court to present his notes for inspection. If the client consents, he then waives his rights to confidentiality. If he does not consent, wherever the court feels that the mental condition of the client is an important issue, disclosure may be ordered (Jakobi and Pratt 1992).

Problems arise more commonly when the patient's right to confidence conflicts with the right of others to information. For example, a patient's family may be considered to have the right to know if the patient is at risk of suicide. In the US, the 1974 Tarasoff decision stated that 'protective privilege ends where public peril begins', meaning that the therapist must warn both potential victims and the authorities if a patient may be dangerous. In the UK, there is no legal obligation to disclose in this situation, but the therapist may feel a moral obligation.

Suicide

Although suicide is no longer a crime, if people are felt to be in danger of self-harm, they can be detained under the Mental Health Act. Furthermore, a mental health professional who does not attempt to safeguard a patient who later commits suicide can be sued for negligence. The ethical dilemma is whether individuals have the right to be autonomous and determine their own lives, or whether a paternalistic approach should be taken, allowing us to protect those who are insufficiently rational to make their own decisions. Szasz (1974) has argued that detaining potential suicides is akin to refusing people permission to emigrate; it is difficult to acccept this analogy, however, since the consequences of the two are very different for the individual concerned and for those who know them.

Termination of treatment

As stated earlier, cost may enter into decisions about this, either abbreviating or lengthening treatment according to the circumstances. Both client and therapist may have cost to consider as well as other factors. Patients may want to prolong the relationship, whilst therapists may want to boost their 'success rates'. Both tendencies need to be avoided by the two parties concerned reaching a consensus. When patients are hospitalised, pressure to release beds and cut costs, or pressure from pro-community care groups may operate to terminate treatment early, which may be no more in the patient's interests than prolonging treatment unnecessarily.

Note that any consideration of ethical issues must of course include those involved in research into mental disorder. These have been discussed in Chapter 8, but can be summarised here as: the need for confidentiality; the need for informed consent to participation; the dilemma of best treatment versus random allocation; and the use of control groups (e.g. placebo conditions and waiting lists). All of these need to be balanced against the need for evaluation as an ethical requirement, and the principle of least harm.

Perhaps this chapter can best be concluded by referring to the idea of risk. Pilgrim and Rogers (1996) refer to this as a two-sided issue: the risk to society posed by patients, and the risk to patients posed by treatments. This seems to summarise the arguments well. These two aspects are illustrated most vividly when it comes to a consideration of community care, which is an important feature of Chapter 10.

Chapter summary

The 1983 Mental Health Act contains several sections which permit mentally disordered persons to be compulsorily detained and treated. Apart from emergency treatment, all treatments require the patient's consent. As well as loss of liberty and other rights, stigmatisation, institutionalisation and mistreatment may result from commitment. In the sphere of criminal law, competence to stand trial and the insanity defence are the main consequences.

Ethical issues also arise in diagnosis, where both purposeful and non-purposeful misdiagnosis may occur. Where treatment is concerned, choice, duration, effectiveness, goals and the type of therapy all raise ethical points. Sexual abuse, sexism, cultural issues, confidentiality, suicide and treatment termination must also be considered carefully.

Review exercise

Draw up a table to summarise the main ethical issues arising from the Mental Health Act, and the diagnosis and treatment of mental disorder.

Sample essay

(a) Describe somatic approaches to the treatment of mental disorder. (12 marks)

(b) Assess these approaches in terms of the ethical implications they raise. (12 marks)   [AEB June 1997]

Further reading

Pilgrim, D. and Rogers, A. (1996) 'Two notions of risk in mental health debates', in T. Heller *et. al. Mental Health Matters*, Milton Keynes: Oxford University Press. (Provides powerful ethical commentary on the therapy industry.)

Illich, I. (1976) *Medical Nemesis*, London: Calder & Boyars. (A classic critique of the medicalisation of life and its adverse effects.)

10

Conclusions: clinical practice

 The eclectic approach
Care in the community
The case against therapy

The eclectic approach

Our exploration of the different types of treatments and therapies for mental disorder has revealed a very wide range of possibilities. Evaluation has suggested that there are both good points and weaknesses associated with them all. How, then, can practitioners make choices between them?

The most popular single option is the **eclectic approach**, adopted by 40 per cent of therapists (Hock 1992). This means choosing the therapy which is most appropriate for a particular client. This choice may be based on theoretical considerations, cost and length of treatment, availability of trained therapists and the estimated effectiveness of the treatment for the disorder concerned (Dallos and Cullen 1990).

It is still necessary to formalise the system which is used for doing this, and therefore Shapiro (1985) has proposed the **scientist-practitioner model** of clinical practice. According to this, the clinical practitioner needs to adopt a scientific approach to working with clients. Dallos and Cullen (1990: 752) suggest that this should involve 'clear descriptions of problems, the formulation of alternative hypotheses guided by psychological knowledge, and the testing of hypotheses by observation, monitoring and other forms of assessment of alternative treatments'. This means that not only should psychological theories and research be considered when choosing a test, but that each individual case needs to be analysed in terms of its unique combination of causes and symptoms. Only then can an appropriate treatment be decided upon, evaluated and adjusted to suit.

An important component of this approach is **progressive hypothesising**, whereby hypotheses based on an initial assessment may lead to particular treatments being chosen; progress made will then be monitored and hypotheses and treatments adjusted. This can be repeated as many times as necessary before treatment is concluded and the outcome finally evaluated on the basis of both objective measures such as observation and the client's subjective reports. The process is illustrated in Figure 10.1.

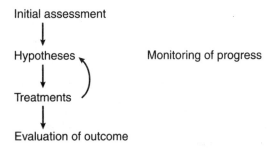

Figure 10.1   **Progressive hypothesising**

The importance of this approach can be seen particularly clearly when it is considered that the features of a mental disorder tend to change over time; different models and treatments may therefore be appropriate at different stages. Using depression as an example, Tyrer and Steinberg (1987) have identified four such stages:

Stages in the course of mental disorder

1 At the *stage of disintegration*, when a crisis strikes, the medical model may be an appropriate one, leading to swift action in the form of hospitalisation and drug treatment.

2 At the *stage of behaviour change*, where social withdrawal may be the key problem, the learning model may be appropriate with its focus on dealing with symptoms using behaviour therapy and behaviour modification.

3 At the *stage of symptoms*, where lack of interest in life may be the principal issue, a psychodynamic model may be useful and psychoanalysis will be the treatment of choice.

4 At the *stage of emotional distress*, where feelings are disrupted and negative, a social model may be employed, leading to a focus on humanistic therapy to increase social contacts and bring about a change in lifestyle. Following this approach, treatment may move from somatic to humanistic throughout the course of the disorder. If the focus were on prevention rather than treatment, then intervention would begin with humanistic approaches instead.

Evaluation

According to Dallos and Cullen (1990), the scientist-practitioner model has two main advantages:

- it prompts clinicians to reassess continually their assumptions and choice of treatment
- it gives clinicians a framework into which to organise the information which they have accumulated

However, this model is not without its critics in practice. For example, Parry (1996) points out that research has had no major effect on practice in the last forty years. Exposure therapy, for instance, has been established to be the best first choice for the treatment of phobias, but the NHS does not have sufficient trained staff to provide it.

As well as the issue of funding, Parry suggests that the links between research and practice could be improved in two ways:

1   Designing practitioner-friendly research. If research were more realistic, better-designed and more available to practitioners (for example by being published in more appropriate journals), then it would be utilised more fully. It is also important that any changes observed in research are clinically as well as statistically significant, leading to noticeable improvements in the disorder concerned (Jacobson and Truax 1991).

2   Developing research-friendly practitioners. If practitioners had more time to study and carry out their own research, they may be more receptive to findings and better able to apply the scientist-practitioner model.

Care in the community

The issues of stigmatisation and institutionalisation have been raised by critics of mental hospitals such as Goffman (1961: 309), from whom the following quote is taken:

> The patient is not the only one, it seems, who declines to view his trouble as simply a type of sickness to be treated and then forgotten. Once he has a record of having been in a mental hospital, the public at large, both formally and informally, in terms of day-to-day social treatment, considers him to be set apart; they place a stigma on him

This has led some writers to suggest that hospitals are not the most appropriate place for people who suffer from mental disorder, and that care in the community may be a better option.

In 1989 a government white paper entitled 'Caring for People' suggested that community care should be provided by social services departments for people with mental health problems. This has led to a reduction in hospitalisation; for example, in 1990, 57,000 hospital beds were available for the mentally ill, compared with 120,000 in 1966. It has also led to the discharge of many long-stay patients into the community. Over half a million people have been discharged in the USA and UK since the 1950s. There is therefore a range of community care being provided under the scheme, including:

- *Residential support*. This varies from high-security units to nursing homes with 24-hour nursing care, unstaffed group houses and ordinary housing. Short-term acute units are provided for those at risk, and crisis accommodation for overnight stays.
- *Day care*. This includes the provision of drop-in community mental health centres, support groups, employment schemes and day hospitals for outpatient treatment or day care while family members are out at work.
- *Home-based care* includes visits from community mental health staff.

Since its inception, the care in the community programme has been controversial.

Evaluation

On the *positive* side, care in the community:

- prevents institutionalisation and dependency.
- may lead to faster recovery since problems are being faced in the environment in which they occurred; patients have to learn to cope with the practical problems of everyday life.
- prevents learning of disordered behaviours from others, as could occur in an institution where people are grouped together and isolated from the rest of society.
- reduces the likelihood of labelling, since patients do not spend time in the 'loony bin' or the 'funny farm'.
- may lead to a reduction in stigmatisation since the public in general will become more familiar with mental disorder.
- means that patients do not have to be uprooted by being moved a long way away from home for treatment (as used to happen frequently with the old hospital system).
- reduces difficulties of reintegrating patients into the community afterwards, and the need for relearning life skills.

However, there are also *negative* aspects to the programme, such as:

- the burden of care may simply be transferred to the patients' families.

- patients may suffer opposition and hostility from local residents (the **NIMBY** – Not In My Back Yard – problem, whereby people may not disapprove of community hostels, etc., provided they do not have to live next door to one).
- specialist staff and treatment may be less readily available if needed.
- inadequate provision could lead to patient deterioration, home-lessness, loneliness, neglect, drug abuse, etc.
- there is an increased burden on the local social services depart-ments and ratepayers to fund units and provide staff.
- the issue of safety of patients and members of the public. This has been a controversial area as a result of media reports of cases of suicide and attacks on the public, so we shall expand on this issue.

   According to Pilgrim and Rogers (1996) 'the great majority of people with a psychiatric diagnosis are never violent, and most of the violence in society is not committed by people with a psychi-atric diagnosis'. The issue may have been exaggerated by reporting biases, since psychiatric reports are often requested where there is violence; thus a psychiatric history may lead to attributing the violence to mental disorder, even though it was not responsible for the violence observed at that particular point in time.

A key issue is the ability of clinicians to predict whether or not patients are likely to be violent. A study by *Lidz et al.* (1993) found that clinicians were better than chance at predicting violence by male patients, but not females. In 1996, a Confidential Inquiry into Homicides and Suicides by Mentally Ill People was published. None of the 100 recorded cases was committed by a patient discharged from a long-stay mental hospital into the community. Another study by Dayson (1993) found that out of 278 patients followed up for a year after discharge, only two were involved in violent offences, and one of these had attacked his father rather than a stranger. So the overall risk, especially to non-relatives, appears to be very low.

Evaluation studies of community care have also been carried out. Meltzer *et al.* (1991) followed up 140 schizophrenics after their discharge from a London acute unit. After one year, four had died, 50 per cent were functioning poorly and 10 per cent were employed. Many lived in deprived circumstances, and services were poorly co-ordinated. Anderson *et al.* (1993) looked at long-stay patients, and found that their quality of life and satisfaction increased after a move to residential care. Muijen *et al.* (1994), however, found that community care produces only slightly better outcomes in terms of psychiatric symptoms and social functioning. Thus the results appear to indicate that the users may have a positive response in terms of satisfaction and engagement with services, but this is not necessarily reflected in objective measures of functioning.

Before leaving the issue of community care, it is instructive to consider another version of this approach, offered by the town of Geel in Belgium. This is outlined in Case study 10.1.

Case study 10.1: Community care in Geel

This community has had a tradition of care since 1250, and operates a system whereby psychiatric patients are placed with local families, with support being provided by the local psychiatric hospital. Both families and patients are strictly selected; 3,736 patients were being cared for in this way by 1938. The families regard it as a legitimate business, but have a strict traditional code regarding its operation (e.g. patients are regarded as family members, and will be 'passed on' to the children if the parents die) and plenty of social support is available from other families. No major incidents or disturbances have been reported, and many patients are able to participate in normal activities; 40 per cent, for example, do the family's shopping (Sedgwick 1982).

Draw up a table to show the advantages and disadvantages of community care. Incorporate evidence to back up your points (this may come from other chapters in the book where appropriate).

Progress exercise

The case against therapy

Finally, we need to consider the argument about whether in practice there is a place for therapy at all. In earlier chapters we have noted that psychotherapy does not always improve the condition of those who receive it; we have also noted that proponents of the socio-cultural model feel that it may be inappropriate altogether, as it does not address the real problems. Three major critics of the use of therapy are Howarth, Masson and Smail, and we will explore their arguments here.

Howarth (1989) rests his argument on the finding that, regardless of the type of therapy used, the outcome for clients is similar (see Chapter 8). There is also evidence that training of therapists does not improve their effectiveness (Berman and Norton 1985). Howarth (1989: 150) therefore concludes from this evidence that 'psychotherapists do not know what they are doing and cannot train others to do it'. In addition to this, there is the evidence that therapy may damage clients. A study by Mair (1997), reported in Chapter 8, demonstrates this well. Another example is the study by McCord (1978), who traced 250 treated clients and 250 matched controls thirty years after the termination of their five-year course of treatment with Rogerian counselling. Although 80 per cent of the treatment group thought that they had benefited, they were actually doing less well than the controls in terms of employment, criminal and health records.

Masson (1988) uses an exploration of Freudian and Jungian psychoanalytic therapy, and the humanistic approaches of Perls and Rogers, to attack what he sees as a corrupt process. His premise is that the therapist, by virtue of his/her position, is bound to act in ways that 'diminish the dignity, autonomy and freedom of the person who comes for help' (1988: 24). According to Masson, 'Every therapy I have examined in this book…displays a lack of interest in social injustice. Each shows a lack of interest in physical and sexual abuse. Each shows an implicit acceptance of the political status quo' (1988: 285).

Smail (1987: 57) has proposed similarly that therapy is oppressive, in his statement that 'Psychology's most significant contribution to modern society is less scientific or therapeutic than managerial' . The problem with therapy in his view is that it focuses on the individual, and attempts to bring about change in that individual by providing a micro-environment in which change is possible. Rather than employing such a process to fit individuals into our existing social structures, he suggests that what is needed is more research into appropriate social structures and ways of living. 'Unless our society *does* mend its ways we may expect no improvement to occur in our private lives' (1987: 157); 'we suffer pain, therefore we do damage to each other, and we shall continue to suffer pain as long as we continue to do the damage' (1987: 1).

As with other health issues addressed in the government's 'Health of the Nation' policy paper, it is clear that prevention may be a better approach than treatment, Here Smail is backed up by Busfield (1996: 141), who argues that 'the absence of preventive social intervention is usually a matter of the lack of political will, and not of the deficiencies of existing knowledge'. It is up to the state, then, which has the power to initiate and co-ordinate such radical social interventions as these writers propose, to decide whether clinical psychology, as well as care, should be given back to the community.

Chapter summary

In this chapter we have considered the ways in which psychological treatments for mental disorders are applied in practice. We have looked at the eclectic approach, and its reliance on the scientist-practitioner model to create a more scientific, research-based approach to treatment. The more recent development of care in the community has been described and evaluated, and finally the case for and against therapy has been underlined by presenting the views of three writers who do not accept its utility, and propose preventative social measures instead.

Use the words given below to fill in the blanks in the passage. Use each word once only.

satisfaction; political; eclectic; residential; prevent; research; practitioner; hypothesising; stage; harmful; community; home; safety

Clinical practice often employs an —— approach to therapy choice, tailoring the treatment to the client. According to the scientist—— model, this needs to be done by a process of progressive —— and evaluation of the outcome of treatment. The treatment used may also differ according to the —— that the disorder has reached. Linking practice with —— is essential if this process is to work well. Care in the —— has been introduced gradually and provides —— support, daycare and ——based care. Where services are well co-ordinated it results in more user ——. The main problem is the fear about public —— that results. However, some influential writers feel that therapy can be —— and that only social and —— change will help to —— mental disorder.

The answers are as follows: eclectic; practitioner; hypothesising; stage; research; community; residential; home; satisfaction; safety; harmful; political; prevent.

Further reading

Busfield, J. (1996) 'Professionals, the state and the development of mental health policy', in T. Heller *et al.* (eds) *Mental Health Matters*, Milton Keynes: Oxford University Press. (Employs a historical approach to provide an outspoken critique of policy-making.)

Dryden, W. and Feltham, C. (eds) (1992) *Psychotherapy and its Discontents*, Milton Keynes: Oxford University Press. (A collection of papers presenting the debate for and against therapy.)

Smail, D. (1986) *Taking Care: An Alternative To Therapy*, London: Dent. (An analysis of the societal origins of personal distress and an advocacy of care rather than therapy. Powerful reading.)

Smail, D. (1991) 'Towards a radical environmentalist psychology of help', *The Psychologist* 2: 61–65. (A concise paper which outlines proposals for changing the environment rather than those who inhabit it.)

11

Study aids

IMPROVING YOUR ESSAY WRITING SKILLS

At this point in the book you have acquired the knowledge necessary to tackle the exam itself. Answering exam questions is a skill which this chapter shows you how to improve. Examiners have some ideas about what goes wrong in exams. Most importantly, students do not provide the kind of evidence the examiner is looking for. A grade 'C' answer is typically accurate but has limited detail and commentary, and it is reasonably constructed. To lift such an answer to a grade 'A' or 'B' may require no more than fuller detail, better use of material and a coherent organisation. By studying the essays presented in this chapter, and the examiner's comments, you can learn how to turn your grade 'C' answer into grade 'A'. Please note that marks given by the examiner in the practice essays should be used as a guide only and are not definitive. They represent the 'raw marks' given by an AEB examiner. That is, the marks the examiner would give to the examining board based on a total of 24 marks per question broken down into Skill A (description) and Skill B (evaluation). Tables showing this scheme are in Appendix C of Paul Humphreys' title in this series, *Exam Success in AEB Psychology*. They may not be the marks given on the examination certificate received ultimately by the student because all examining boards are required to use a common standardised system called the Uniform Mark Scale (UMS) which adjusts all raw scores to a single standard acceptable to all examining boards.

The essays are about the length a student would be able to write in 35–40 minutes (leaving you extra time for planning and checking). Each essay is followed by detailed comments about its strengths and weaknesses. The most common problems to look out for are:

- Failure to answer the question set and presenting 'one written during your course'.
- A lack of evaluation, or commentary – many weak essays suffer from this.
- Too much evaluation and not enough description. Description is vital in demonstrating your knowledge and understanding of the selected topic.
- Writing 'everything you know' in the hope that something will get credit. Excellence is displayed through selectivity, and therefore improvements can often be made by *removing* material which is irrelevant to the question set.

For more ideas on how to write good essays you should consult *Exam Success in AEB Psychology* (Paul Humphreys) in this series.

Practice essay 1

Critically consider the effectiveness of any two types of therapies/treatments for psychological disorders. (24 marks)
[AEB 1998]

Starting point: 'Critically consider' is a term which requires candidates to demonstrate knowledge and understanding of the effectiveness of the two treatments chosen, and to show an awareness of the strengths and weaknesses of the evidence used to evaluate those treatments. An examiner would therefore be looking for the selection of two appropriate treatments, presentation of comments and key studies on treatment outcomes, and a balanced evaluation of those studies.

A psychological disorder is defined as being a disorder that prevents your mind from functioning in the correct manner that is needed for everyday functioning. There are 5 main types of therapies available for the treatment of psychological disorders: medical (somatic), humanistic, behavioural, psychodynamic and cognitive-behavioural. Behavioural and somatic will be discussed in this essay. The behavioural model of treatment of psychological disorders is based on the assumption that disorders are learned processes. They state that they are learned in the same way that we learn to ride a bike. There are two parts to the behavioural model. One is based on classical conditioning and the other on operant.

Systematic desensitisation states that there are levels in fear arousal. The method assumes that if one is exposed to fear then the physiological response cannot continue for a sustained period of time. The client is exposed to different fear levels until eventually they are no longer afraid. The technique is obviously used for phobias. Wolpe (1978) criticised this technique by stating that there are strong neurotic forces in society that can change the repair done. Therefore he invented 'thought stopping'; every time the participant thinks about a fear they tell themselves to stop.

Another technique derived from classical conditioning is flooding – this technique is also used for fears and phobias. The patient is exposed to their worst fear in the view that after a certain period of time their body cannot sustain the heightened activity that occurs in phobia states. Gradually the patient is expected to become accustomed to the process. The technique can be introduced in vitro (artificial status) or vivo (real life). However, due to ethical considerations for the participant the technique normally occurs in vitro.

The classical conditioning methods have a high success rate for phobias and fears, however that is a narrow range of cures. The methods are often criticised for ethics as the patient is put under a great deal of stress.

The operant conditioning methods include token economy; this normally occurs in institutions. The patient is rewarded in tokens for things that are done correctly. It can be used for obsessive-compulsive disorder, anxiety disorders, phobias and even depression. However, the technique may not be effective outside the institution as the patient may be expecting rewards and due to the lack of rewards may relapse.

Social skills training (Bandura 1989) is another method of operant conditioning. It is effective with a range of disorders and does not have as high a relapse rate as token economy.

Behavioural therapies are effective whilst the institution or therapist is around, However, once out of therapy they are not very successful. There also may be other factors that influence the abnormality of patients not just learned behaviour. It has also been found that the attention of a token economy can produce recovery not actually the tokens themselves.

The medical model (somatic) assumes that psychological disorders are of a physiological origin, the same as a physiological disorder.

Electroconvulsive therapy is used for bipolar depression and manic depressive psychosis. It was introduced in the 1930's and soon after gained a bad name for the harm that it caused. In the modern age the patient is given an anaesthetic and they rarely feel a thing. Its aim is to influence the serotonin levels in the brain and to produce normal levels through electric shock. It has a reasonable success rate, although it is a dangerous procedure. Patients have been known to have heart attacks due to it. It is legal to give a patient ECT without their consent, which may promote ethical issues.

Psychosurgery is used in depression and schizophrenia. Sometimes it is used in other conditions when all other treatments fail. It involves modifying the cerebral cortex of the brain. The advantage of it is that drugs do not have to be taken and the patient can continue as normal. The drawbacks of the technique are that it is highly dangerous and the process is irreversible.

The medical model also provides drugs for patients. There are 4 main types available: anti-anxiety, anti-psychotic, anti-depressant and a type for mania. Drugs have advantages in that they are effective at treating almost any disorder. They are also available for any patient regardless of their intelligence or wealth and they are readily available. However, their drawbacks include dependency and side effects.

The somatic model is an effective treatment in that it provides many people with an opportunity to function normally. However, it is not a cure, it simply balances out chemicals that are imbalanced for an unknown reason.

Both the behavioural and somatic models are effective in their own way. Both have major drawbacks, but the main thing is that both therapies allow people to function normally.

Examiner's comments

This is a reasonably constructed answer which shows some psychological knowledge, but displays more breadth than depth. The chief weakness is the complete absence of any empirical studies. The other major shortcoming is an overemphasis on a description of the therapies rather than their effectiveness (the focal point of the question). The answer starts well with an attempt at definition (although the definition offered is rather weak), and sets the scene well by naming the different models, indicating clearly which treatments are going to be discussed.

The section on behavioural approaches is limited in range and very vague (and/or inaccurate) regarding both theories and techniques. Much of the material that is included is not essential to answer the question. For example, evaluative points are not well elaborated and there is no reference to research evidence. Somatic approaches are not accurately described or evaluated, and again there is no reference to research.

The total mark for this question is about 5 (description) + around 4 (evaulation) = 9/24 (likely to be equivalent to a grade 'E' at A-level). In this case it would appear that the candidate does not know this area sufficiently well to provide accurate description and detailed evaluation. For example, the important issue of ethics could be explained, particularly as regards informed consent. The nature of the side effects associated with different drugs could also be outlined. Key studies of the effectiveness of therapy, such as that by Smith *et al.*, could also be included. These would then provide an opportunity to discuss the difficulties of carrying out such research, such as placebo effects, spontaneous remission, how to define a cure, etc. Both breadth and depth of this answer would then be improved.

Practice essay 2

Discuss the use of two cognitive-behavioural therapies in the treatment of psychological disorders. (24 marks)

[AEB 1998]

Starting point: 'Discuss' is a term which requires the candidate to both describe and evaluate the two chosen therapies. The description needs to detail the ways the named therapies are used, and can include the rationale behind them, the techniques involved and the disorders they are used to treat. The evaluation can include a discussion of how effective the therapy is (as shown by outcome research, for example), as well as how ethical it is (e.g. the extent to which control is exerted by the therapist) and how practical it is (e.g. cost-effectiveness, availability).

Candidate's answer

Cognitive behavioural therapies were founded by Ellis, believing that with the correct help, thoughts, feelings and beliefs could be rationalised with the help of a trained therapist. The concept then developed of Rational Emotive Behavioural Therapy (REBT), a technique devised believing that cognition and behaviour play a part in evaluating. Anxiety, stress and depression are all thought to be psychological disorders. Cognitive therapies help to identify the source relating to the particular symptom, then help to alleviate it.

The ABC model devised by Ellis would be one such strategy. Here the client is shown a programme. The client and therapist then work through this programme identifying where ideas could be perceived differently. The plan is made up of: A – Activating Event; B – Beliefs about A; C – Consequences of B. The activating event could be 'sitting a psychology exam'. Beliefs could either be positive (i.e. have tried and maybe next time revise and work a little harder) or negative thoughts (i.e. I'm no good at this, I should have taken biology). The consequences then depict the thoughts we felt previously, i.e. 'there is always another time' or 'I shall finish college'.

Meichenbaum and Cameron also devised a programme (stress inoculation programme) which consists of three components: conceptualisation; skills training and rehearsal; application and follow-up. Conceptualisation is to help identify the particular source of stress. Stress training and rehearsal deals with alleviating the stress, identifying the skills necessary in dealing with the stressor, and practising such strategies. And finally application is applying such techniques in a relaxed and therapeutic environment, where help is available if any problems arise.

Therapies such as those mentioned above do of course work if the patient/client is able to self-evaluate. Patients with schizophrenia who have lost touch with the real world would find these therapies difficult. In about 70% of patients undertaking any behavioural therapy the findings are that they are effective, although the critics would say that there are too many variables to be valid.

These programmes such as Ellis' and Meichenbaum and Cameron's have been used in a variety of settings, i.e. NHS, Social Services and work places (stress management). Although not as cheap and as quick as somatic treatments (i.e. drugs, ECT), they are seen to have no serious side-effects. Unlike psychodynamic approaches where the patient has to be in the best of health to undergo regression, these concentrate on cognitions and behaviour, helping patients to help themselves. As with all therapies, maybe an eclectic approach would be the answer.

Examiner's comments

This essay is well-structured in terms of having a clear introduction, a description of the two therapies and an evaluation section. It starts well with an explanation of the basis of cognitive-behavioural therapy, although little detail is provided and there are some inaccuracies. For example, the descriptions of Ellis' REBT and Meichenbaum's Stress Inoculation approach are clear if limited and lacking in depth. The evaluation section makes some sound points, but they could be better elaborated and the range of issues discussed could be broadened. No outcome research is presented, which is a serious omission in a question of this nature.

The final mark for this question is about 12–14/24 (likely to be equivalent to a grade 'C' at A-level). What the candidate presents is generally accurate, but lacks detail. To improve on this, more information needs to be included on techniques used in such therapies, e.g. the use of 'homework' and 'thought-stopping', and the ways in which these techniques are underpinned by cognitive-behavioural theories.

Ethical and practical considerations could be included, as could outcome studies such as that of Clark (1992) – described in this chapter. These outcome studies can in turn be criticised, drawing on material presented in Chapters 7 and 8. With questions of this type, the candidate needs to bear both parts of the question in mind when selecting which therapies to discuss. In this case, the candidate has chosen two which can be described fairly well, but are not associated with any specific evaluation – just general comments about cognitive-behavioural therapy.

KEY RESEARCH SUMMARY

In this section we will be looking at short summaries of three key papers which have been referred to in the course of this book. You may find it helpful to make a very brief summary of your own for each, including just one or two key points and a note about which of the areas covered in the book the study is most relevant to. Remember that case studies are also an important form of research in atypical psychology, and examples of these have been given throughout the book.

Article 1

The Token Economy, **by T. Allyon and N. Arzin, New York: Appleton Century Crofts (1968)**

Notes

This is an innovative piece of research into the use of behaviour therapy with institutionalised psychotic patients, which introduced the 'token economy' to psychology. The token economy system has since been successfully applied in a wide range of psychiatric and non-psychiatric situations. Although the system has been criticised for being manipulative, and for the likelihood of relapse when reinforcement is withdrawn, its contribution to practice cannot be underestimated.

Summary

The aim of this study was to reinforce behaviours in psychotic hospital patients. Tokens and other secondary (or learnt) reinforcers were used to ensure that appropriate behaviour was followed rapidly by reinforcement, since this is when reinforcement is most effective. Behaviours such as cleaning floors were chosen to reinforce because they were felt to be useful to the patient, and because they were easy to measure objectively. Reinforcers were selected that were effective and were part of the natural environment on the ward, e.g. choice of rooms and chairs, a walk in the grounds, and opportunities for social interaction. The range of reinforcers is shown in Table 11.1.

Table 11.1 Range of reinforcers available for tokens

Contact with other patients	Examples include choice of bedroom (ranged from 0–30 tokens), choice of eating group (1 token), choice of personal chair (1 token) and opportunity to have a personal cabinet (2 tokens).
Opportunity to leave the ward	Examples ranged from a 20 minute walk in grounds (2 tokens) to a trip to town (100 tokens)
Private interaction with staff	This ranged from 1 token per minute to interact with ward staff to 100 tokens for an audience with a social worker.
Leisure opportunities	Watching a film on the ward would cost 1 token; choice of TV programme would be 3 tokens.
Personal belongings	Consumables cost up to 5 tokens, toiletries up to 10, clothing up to 400 and any special requests such as pot plants up to 50. Stuffed animals were apparently very popular!

All experiments carried out followed an A-B-A design (baseline-intervention-baseline), so that patients served as their own controls. In all, six experiments were carried out on up to forty-four patients (although some experiments involved as few as five patients). The patients were mostly schizophrenics, although there were a few mental defectives. They had been hospitalised for between one and thirty-seven years.

Results showed that the introduction of reinforcement procedures, whereby tokens were provided for carrying out desired behaviours, led to increased performance of those behaviours. Performance fell again when the tokens were no longer provided. The reinforcers found to be the most effective differed according to individual preferences and related to behaviours that were already frequent in the patient's repertoire, e.g. privacy behaviours. The procedure was even effective in chronic cases, but was ineffective in eight patients who showed few behaviours other than eating and sleeping and therefore provided few that could be used as reinforcers. The conclusion was that such procedures could be used to encourage psychotic patients to function independently.

Article 2

'Treating panic attacks', by D. Clark, *The Psychologist* 6: 73–74 (1993)

Notes

This is a summary of an important series of studies by the author into the cognitive basis and treatment of panic disorders. It provides a good example of the way that careful research can establish links between a model and the most effective form of treatment for a particular disorder.

Summary

Panic attacks involve experiencing intense bodily sensations associated with a panic state, leading early researchers to think that the disorder was physiologically based. A surge of autonomic arousal appears to come out of nowhere, without a trigger, producing a pounding heart, shortness of breath and feelings of extreme anxiety. According to Clark, the key problem is in fact a thought disorder which leads patients to misinterpret bodily feedback as an indicator of severe physical problems such as a heart attack or suffocation. Research has shown that such patients are more likely than controls to interpret bodily sensations as indicative of the onset of severe problems. This leads them to be hypervigilant and scan the body for danger signs, as well as avoiding carrying out behaviours such as exercise, which could initiate such sensations. Even reading word pairs such as 'breathless–suffocate' would be enough to trigger an attack.

Controlled trials in several countries on the treatment of such cases with cognitive therapy have indicated that the therapy has 90 per cent effectiveness in treating panic disorder. The cognitive approach entails: identification of the catastrophic interpretations of bodily signals; generation of alternative responses; and testing the correctness of alternatives by discussion and behavioural experiments (e.g. asking clients to do something other than what they would normally do when they feel an attack coming on – doing press-ups instead of sitting down quickly, for instance).

An evaluation study compared CBT, applied relaxation training, a waiting list control and a chemotherapy group (who were given the antidepressant imipramine over a period of six months). Patients were asked to assess the credibility of the treatment in all treatment conditions. It was found that all conditions were equal in terms of whether the patients thought it was logical, likely to work and whether they would recommend it to a friend. Compared with the control group (waiting list), all three treatment groups were effective as measured by the number of attacks recorded in a panic diary. CBT was the most effective in inducing change in cognitions and reducing the frequency of panic attacks. After three months, 90 per cent of the CBT group were cured, compared to 50 per cent of the chemotherapy group (this latter group also showed a relapse after withdrawal of the drug). Spontaneous recovery in the waiting list group was only found in 7 per cent of cases. A meta-analysis of eight controlled trials showed that 83 per cent of the CBT patients remained panic-free on follow-up, hence CBT would appear to be the most effective treatment for this disorder.

Article 3

'Drugs and psychological treatments for agoraphobia/panic and obsessive-compulsive disorders: a review', by I. Marks and G. O'Sullivan, *British Journal of Psychiatry* 153: 650–58 (1988)

Notes

This is a classic review paper which compares a wide range of different treatments and treatment combinations for two types of neurotic disorder. Its importance lies in the discussion about how to establish whether a treatment has been effective and the detailed listing of important considerations when making treatment decisions.

Summar

The most common treatments for the disorders mentioned in the title were reviewed in this study. The measures of their effectiveness were as follows:

1   Specificity – which symptoms improve.
2   Size – how much improvement is shown.
3   Delay – how long before there is improvement.
4   Duration of improvement – both short- and long-term.
5   Costs – e.g. side effects of treatment.
6   Interactions with other treatments.
7   Trade-offs relative to other treatments.

The psychological treatment concerned was exposure treatment, whereby patients are encouraged to maintain contact with the feared object or the stimulus that provokes rituals. This was reviewed on the basis of the publication by Marks (1987), and was found to be the most helpful psychological intervention for these disorders. The improvement shown by patients is such that they can maintain normal lives after treatment, and it begins within a few hours of the initiation of treatment. After treatment stops, it can be maintained for up to eight years, with booster treatments if relapse occurs. The only drawback is that it is uncomfortable for patients at first.

In order to assess drug treatments, seventeen drug studies were reviewed, covering a range of different antidepressant drugs such as the tricyclic imipramine and the monoamine oxidase inhibitors (MAOIs), as well as tranquillisers such as the benzodiazepines. All of the studies reported had employed placebo controls and double-blind procedures. The drugs were found to be very broad in their effects, influencing many aspects of behaviour, and also took some time to bring about these changes (several weeks in some cases). There were relapse problems, so the changes produced were not lasting, and also side effects such as dependence. The conclusion was that the drugs were not worth trying unless the patients refused or failed in their attempts to participate in exposure therapy, or were suffering from mood disorders in addition to the problems being treated. Treatment decisions were then discussed in terms of six major factors:

1 *Specificity of effects*. Drugs affect other aspects of functioning; exposure does not.
2 *Relative size of the effect*. The effect size is comparable for drugs and exposure treatments in terms of the target symptoms, but exposure also improves work and social adjustment.
3 *Delay in showing improvement*. This varies with the drug taken, some tranquillisers taking effect within minutes, but it can take up to twelve weeks for the maximum effect to be felt with other drugs. The timescale was more variable for exposure; benefits may be noticeable immediately, but it could take months to complete the programme.
4 *Short-term duration of effect*. The effectiveness of drugs may reduce with time even when the drug is still taken.
5 *Long-term duration of effect*. 'There are no data showing that medication has value beyond the point where it is stopped'. Follow-ups after exposure therapy showed that it was still effective up to four to eight years later.
6 *Cost, in terms of effort, finance, side effects and drop-out from treatment*. Exposure involves greater effort from participants than drug therapy. The financial costs of drugs vary according to the type and brand, but they can be high if medication is continued over a long period. Exposure, on the other hand, may only require a few hours of the therapist's time. Many side effects are possible from drug therapy, whereas exposure therapy involves initial anxiety and discomfort which soon reduces. The drop-out rate of 10–30 per cent is similar for the two treatments.

Overall, it was concluded that both treatments could be helpful in the short-term, but that for long-term effectiveness exposure was superior.

Glossary

The first occurrence of each of these terms is highlighted in **bold** type in the main text.

ABC model A model devised by Ellis to illustrate how irrational beliefs can form the basis for mental disorder.

analogue experiment An experiment which uses one phenomenon to represent another.

anorexia nervosa An eating disorder associated with extreme weight loss and fear of becoming obese.

anxiety hierarchy A ranked list of anxiety-producing stimuli used during systematic desensitisation.

anxiolytics Anxiety-reducing drugs, also called tranquillisers.

authenticity Term used by existentialists to refer to the development of individuality and purpose in life.

autism Severe childhood mental disorder involving lack of communication, withdrawal from social contact and restricted range of interests and activities.

automatic thoughts Beck's term for the repetitive, often irrational thoughts that people have about themselves and others.

aversion therapy A form of behaviour therapy which involves associating unpleasant things with stimuli which are to be avoided.

behaviour modification Therapeutic procedures based on operant conditioning.

behaviour shaping The gradual learning of new behaviour during operant conditioning, by reinforcing successive approximations to the desired response.

behaviour therapy General term for therapeutic procedures based on classical conditioning.

between groups comparison design An experimental design which compares the performance of an experimental group with that of a control (no treatment) group.

bipolar disorder A mental disorder involving mood swings between mania and depression.

case study method A type of research method in which the behaviour of one person or a small group is examined in detail, often over a long period of time.

chemotherapy The use of drugs to treat mental disorders.

cingulotomy A brain operation which involves cutting the connections between the prefrontal cortex and the limbic system.

classical conditioning The process of learning to associate a reflex response with a previously neutral stimulus.

cognitive distortions Errors in thinking that lead people with mental disorders to misperceive reality.

cognitive triad A negative view of the self, the present and the future, thought by Beck to be at the root of depression.

conjoint therapy Couple or family therapy in which individuals are seen together by the therapist.

core conditions Three conditions – genuineness, unconditional positive regard and empathic understanding – thought by Rogers to be essential for change to occur during therapy.

correlational method A method of research which attempts to establish whether there are relationships between variables.

cost-benefit analysis The ethical requirement to weigh up the positive and negative features of treatments when making choices between them.

counselling A term for the application of Rogerian techniques to help people who have problems but who are not necessarily suffering from mental disorder.

covert sensitisation A form of aversion therapy in which unpleasant stimuli are imagined rather than real.

dependency Psychological or physiological reliance upon a psychoactive substance.

dependent variable The variable in an experiment which is measured to show the effect of an experimental manipulation.

depression A mood disorder characterised by sadness, negative thoughts, reduced activity and motivation, loss of sleep and appetite.

discrimination A term used in conditioning to refer to the ability to differentiate between similar stimuli.

dissociative identity disorder A syndrome in which an individual has two or more separate personalities, with different behaviours.

dopamine An important neurotransmitter in the central nervous system.

dream interpretation A psychoanalytic technique which aims to uncover the unconscious meanings of dreams.

dreamwork The process of unravelling the symbols employed in dreams in order to reveal the meaning behind them.

DSM IV The fourth edition of the American Psychiatric Association's Diagnostic and Statistical Manual, used to define and classify mental disorder.

eclectic approach Selecting what seems best from a range of different ideas.

electro-convulsive shock therapy (ECT) The induction of convulsions by passing an electric current through the brain, mainly used to treat depression.

emetic A drug used in aversion therapy to induce nausea and vomiting.

empathy The ability to understand and imagine how another person is feeling.

empty chair technique Technique used in Gestalt therapy which requires the client to converse with an absent person as if that person were sitting in an empty chair.

enuresis A disorder involving faulty bladder control, especially during sleep.

epidemiology Study of the frequency and distribution of illness in a population.

equivalence paradox The name given to the similarity in degree of effectiveness of different therapies for mental disorder.

experimental method   A research method in which an independent variable(s) is manipulated and the effect of this on a dependent variable(s) is measured, all other variables being controlled.

exposure therapy   A form of behaviour therapy in which the individual is exposed to the feared object or situation without the possibility of escape.

extinction   The cessation of a learned response when reinforcement is no longer provided.

family therapy   Psychotherapy that is carried out with family members as a group.

flooding   A form of exposure therapy that involves real contact with the feared situation or object.

free association   A technique used in psychoanalysis, in which the patient is encouraged to say whatever comes to mind, without censorship.

functional analysis   A method of ascertaining the conditions responsible for maintaining behaviour, including settings, prompts and consequences.

GABA   An important inhibitory neurotransmitter.

generalisation   The process whereby learned responses may occur in similar forms, and/or to similar stimuli, to those involved in the original learning.

gestalt therapy   A humanistic therapy in which individuals are encouraged to develop greater awareness of themselves as whole beings.

hello-goodbye effect   Describes the way in which a client's reports of symptoms may be distorted at the beginning and at the end of therapy.

hyperactivity   Often associated with Attention Deficit Hyperactivity Disorder, this includes excessive activity of many kinds (verbal and motor), and an inability to delay impulses.

implosion   A type of flooding therapy which involves imagined contact with the feared object/situation.

incidence   The number of new cases of a given disorder which occur in a given population over a given period.

independent variable   The variable which the experimenter manipulates in order to observe the effect it has on another variable.

informed consent   Agreement to participate in research or therapy after being given full information about what is involved, including both costs and benefits.

insanity defence   The plea that an individual is not guilty of committing an illegal act, by reason of insanity at the time of the crime.

insight   The realisation, during the course of psychoanalysis, of the origins of unconscious conflicts and their connection with present mental disorder.

institutionalisation   Inability to cope in the real world, or other negative effects that result from long periods spent in an institution.

latent learning   Learning which may not immediately be shown in behaviour.

law of effect   Principle of learning which states that the effect of a behaviour will determine whether or not it is likely to be repeated.

law of exercise   Principle of learning which states that repetition strengthens associations.

learned helplessness   A state, associated by Seligman with depression, in which apathy results from being unable to escape from an unpleasant situation.

Least Restrictive Alternative   The principle that a sectioned mental patient must be placed in a setting that imposes as few restrictions as possible on his/her freedom.

limbic leucotomy   Brain surgery which isolates the limbic system from the rest of the brain.

mania   A psychotic state in which the individual has high energy levels, great excitement and grandiose ideas.

meta-analysis   A research method which combines the results of several studies, all investigating the same issue.

milieu therapy   A treatment that aims to reduce the effects of institutionalisation by creating an atmosphere of personal responsibility and reducing staff-patient distinctions.

models   Systems of belief, in this context about the causes of mental disorder.

modelling   Therapy based on Bandura's social learning theory, in which clients are exposed to models demonstrating the behaviours they are hoping to imitate.

monoamine oxidase inhibitors   A group of antidepressant drugs that inhibit the action of the enzyme monoamine oxidase and hence increase the available levels of some neurotransmitters.

multiple baseline procedure   An experimental design in which one behaviour of a client is treated whilst another, untreated behaviour acts as a baseline against which to measure treatment effects.

negative practice   A behaviour modification technique which requires the client to repeat the undesirable behaviour as often as possible without rest in a short period.

neuroleptics   Drugs used to treat psychosis, previously known as major tranquillisers.

neurosis   A mental disorder characterised by anxiety but without loss of contact with reality.

neurotransmitters   Chemicals that are involved in communication between neurons in the nervous system.

NIMBY   An acronym for 'Not In My Back Yard', meaning someone who approves of a development as long as it does not affect them personally in an adverse way.

noradrenaline   An important neurotransmitter involved in arousal and mood.

object relations theory   Klein's theory about mental disorder originating in early relationships with others as part and whole objects.

obsessive-compulsive disorder   A form of neurosis in which thoughts or actions become persistent, uncontrollable and interfere with everyday functioning.

operant conditioning   Skinner's theory that learning occurs as a result of reinforcement of responses.

panic disorder   A form of neurosis in which inexplicable feelings of terror and physiological symptoms of fear occur for no apparent reason.

parapraxes   'Slips of the tongue' used in psychoanalysis to gain access to the unconscious. Also known as 'Freudian slips'.

personal construct therapy   The treatment of mental disorder by changing the client's constructs, or ways of interpreting experiences.

personality disorders   A group of mental disorders characterised by ingrained, inflexible, maladaptive traits which impair social functioning.

person-centred therapy   Humanistic therapy based on Rogers' self theory, which aims to place control in the hands of the client rather than the therapist.

phobia   A neurotic disorder which is characterised by irrational, incapacitating fear of an object or situation.

phototherapy   The use of artificial light to treat Seasonal Affective Disorder.

placebo   A treatment which, unknown to the patient, contains no active ingredient and will affect behaviour only as a result of the patient's expectations.

play therapy   Psychodynamic therapy for children which uses play to gain access to the unconscious.

positive conditioning   A behaviour therapy technique which aims to establish a response rather than eliminate one.

prefrontal lobotomy   A form of psychosurgery which involves isolation of the frontal lobes of the cortex.

prevalence   The proportion of the population suffering from a particular disorder at a given point in time.

progressive hypothesising   The process of adjusting hypotheses regarding the best treatment for a disorder according to the progress made by the patient.

psychosis   A severe mental disorder in which the individual loses touch with reality.

psychosurgery   The removal or isolation of brain tissue in order to alleviate mental disorder.

punishment   The presentation of a noxious stimulus in order to reduce the probability of a particular response.

quasi-experiment   An experiment which takes advantage of naturally-occurring changes in an independent variable.

randomised controlled trial   The random allocation of participants to either an experimental or a control group.

random sampling   A sample in which every member of a given population has an equal chance of being included.

rational-emotive therapy   A cognitive therapy based on the theory of Ellis that mental disorder is the result of irrational thoughts and unrealistic goals.

reciprocal inhibition   A procedure used during systematic desensitisation to reduce an unwanted response by pairing it with an antagonistic response, e.g. fear paired with pleasure.

reflection   A technique used in Rogerian therapy which involves the therapist paraphrasing what the client has said in order to check understanding.

reinforcement   A procedure used to strengthen or promote learning.

reliability   Consistency of results in an experiment or agreement between clinicians about diagnosis.

repertory grid   A technique used by Personal Construct therapists to measure change in an individual's constructs during therapy.

resistance   The way that the ego tries to ward off repressed material and prevent it from reaching consciousness during psychodynamic therapy.

reversal design   An experimental design which involves alternating baseline and treatment conditions as time goes on, so that individuals can serve as their own controls.

schizophrenia   A group of severe psychotic disorders involving disturbances in thought, emotions and behaviour, such as hallucinations and delusions.

scientist-practitioner model   The scientific approach to treatment, involving hypothesis-testing and monitoring of response to treatment, as well as forging clear links between research and practice.

script analysis   Monitoring habitual ways of interacting during Transactional Analysis.

Seasonal Affective Disorder   Depressive mood disorder which occurs in summer or winter forms.

sectioning   Confining or treating a person under a section of the Mental Health Act.

selective serotonin re-uptake inhibitors   Drugs which increase the level of available serotonin by preventing its reabsorption after it has been released into the junction between neurons.

self-actualisation   The need of all individuals to realise their full potential.

self-efficacy   The belief that one is capable of acting effectively.

self-instructional training   A cognitive therapy based on Meichenbaum's ideas, which helps clients to change their internal dialogues to more adaptive ones.

serotonin   A neurotransmitter that is involved in depression and mania.

social learning theory   Learning that takes place through observation and imitation of the behaviour of others.

social psychiatry   Therapies based on the existential/socio-cultural model of mental disorder, which aim to change the client's social surroundings as an aid to the development of more adaptive behaviours.

spontaneous remission Improvement in a disorder without any formal treatment.

stigmatisation Marking someone out as a social outcast, for having treatment for mental disorder, for example.

stimulants Drugs which increase alertness, confidence and energy levels.

stimulus satiation A form of behaviour modification which relies on providing excessive amounts of a reinforcer.

successive approximations Behaviours which come closer and closer to what is wanted during operant conditioning.

survey a research method that involves collecting information (e.g. about attitudes) from a large sample of people, often employing a questionnaire.

symptom substitution The argument of psychodynamic theorists that one symptom will simply be replaced by another if the underlying problem is not resolved

systematic desensitisation A behaviour therapy technique which eliminates phobias by gradually introducing the feared object/situation while reciprocally inhibiting the fear response.

Tarasoff decision An American ruling that requires therapists to notify the appropriate persons if they consider that their clients may be dangerous.

tardive dyskinesia A permanent muscular disturbance produced as a side effect by some of the major tranquillisers.

therapeutic alliance The relationship between therapist and client, thought to be the basis for effective therapy.

therapeutic communities Attempts to create alternative, more liberal environments where patients can learn to develop more adaptive ways of functioning through participation in community life.

three systems approach The argument that mental disorder has behavioural, affective/cognitive and physiological components.

token economy A behaviour modification technique where patients are given tokens as rewards for desirable behaviours, which they can exchange at a later time for other items or privileges.

tolerance The need for ever-increasing amounts of a psychoactive substance to produce the same effect.

Tourette's Syndrome   A condition involving involuntary movements, spitting, swearing and shouting.

tranquillisers   Drugs used to reduce tension and anxiety in psychosis and neurosis.

transactional analysis   A humanistic therapy based on the theory of Berne, which analyses interactions in terms of the ego states revealed, either parent, child, or adult.

transcranial magnetic stimulation   The application of magnetic fields to create temporary brain lesions.

transference   In psychodynamic theory, this refers to the way that the client transfers emotions previously directed towards significant others (e.g. the parents) onto the analyst.

transorbital leucotomy   A technique for carrying out lobotomies via the orbit of the eye.

tricyclic antidepressants   A group of antidepressant drugs with a similar chemical structure, all based on molecules with three fused rings.

two-factor model   Mowrer's theory that fear can be learnt through classical conditioning, and avoidance through operant conditioning, creating a phobia.

unconditional positive regard   Providing love and esteem for others without any conditions attached, one of Rogers' core conditions for therapy.

validity   The extent to which a test, an experiment or a diagnosis really represents what it claims to represent.

withdrawal   The unpleasant physiological and psychological reactions that occur when someone suddenly stops taking a psychoactive substance.

working through   The psychodynamic process by which the client comes to terms with repressed conflicts and accepts the analyst's interpretations.

YAVIS syndrome   The type of people most suited to psychodynamic therapy – young, attractive, verbal, intelligent, successful.

Bibliography

Allen, M. G. (1976) 'Twin studies of affective illness', *Archives of General Psychiatry* 35, 1476–8.

Alloy. L. B. and Abramson, L. Y. (1979) 'Judgement of contingency in depressed and non-depressed students: Sadder but wiser?', *Journal of Experimental Psychology*: General 108, 441–85.

Allyon, T. and Azrin, N. (1965) 'The measurement and reinforcement of behaviour of psychotics', *Journal of the Experimental Analysis of Behaviour* 8, 357–83.

Allyon, T. and Azrin, N. (1968) *The Token Economy: A Motivational System for Therapy and Rehabilitation*, New York: Appleton Century Crofts.

Anderson, J. *et al.* (1993) 'The TAPS project 13: clinical and social outcomes of long-stay psychiatric patients after one year in the community', *British Journal of Psychiatry* 162, 42–55.

Anderson, I. and Tomenson, B. (1995) 'Treatment discontinuation with SSRI's compared with tricyclic antidepressants: a meta-analysis', *British Medical Journal* 310, 1433–8.

Andrews, G. (1991) 'The evaluation of psychotherapy', *Current Opinions of Psychotherapy* 4, 379–83.

Ashurst, P. and Ward, D. (1983) *An Evaluation of Counselling in General Practice*, Final Report of the Leverhulme Counselling Project.

Bachrach, A. *et al.* (1965) 'The control of eating behaviour in an anorexic by operant conditioning', in L. Ullman and L. Krasner (eds) *Case Studies in Behaviour Modification*, New York: Holt, Rinehart and Winston.

Baer *et al.* (1995) cited in N. Carlson and W. Buskist, *Psychology: The Science of Behaviour*, Allyn & Bacon, 1997.

Bandura, A. (1969) *Principles of Behaviour Modification*, NY: Rinehart & Winston.

Bandura, A. (1971) *Social learning theory*, Morristown, NJ: General Learning Press.

Bandura, A. (1977) 'Self-efficacy: towards a unifying theory of behaviour change', *Psychology Review* 84, 191–215.

Barnes, M. and Berke, J. (1982) *Mary Barnes*, Harmondsworth: Penguin.

Baron, R. A. (1989) *Psychology: The Essential Science*, London: Allyn & Bacon.

Bateson, G. *et al.* (1956) 'Toward a theory of schizophrenia', *Behavioural Science* 1, 251–64.

Beail, N. and Parker, S. (1991) 'Group fixed-role therapy: a clinical application', *International Journal of Personal Construct Psychology* 4, 85–95.

Bean, P. and Mounser, P. (1993) *Discharge From Mental Hospitals*, London: Macmillan.

Beck, A. T. (1963) *Depression: Clinical, experimental and theoretical aspects*, NY: Harper & Row.

Beck, A. T. (1967) *Depression: Causes and Treatment*, Philadelphia: University of Philadelphia Press.

Beck, A. T. and Emery, G. (1985) *Anxiety disorders and phobias: a cognitive perspective*, New York: Basic books.

Beck, A. T. and Freeman, A. (1990) *Cognitive Therapy of Personality Disorders*, New York: Guilford.

Beck, A. T. *et al.* (1979) *Cognitive Therapy of Depression*, New York: Guilford.

Benton (1981), cited in R. D. Gross, *Psychology: The science of mind and behaviour*, London: Hodder & Stoughton, 1992.

Bergin, A. E. (1971) 'The evaluation of therapeutic outcomes', in A. E. Bergin and S. L. Garfield (eds), *Handbook of Psychotherapy and Behaviour Change*, NY: Wiley.

Bergin, A. E. and Lambert, M. J. (1978) 'The evaluation of therapeutic outcomes', in S. A. Garfield and A. E. Bergin (eds), *Handbook of Psychotherapy and Behaviour Change*, NY: Wiley.

Berman, J. and Norton, N. (1985) 'Does professional training make a therapist more effective?', *Psychological Bulletin* 98, 401–7.

Berne, E. (1964) *Games People Play*, NY: Grove Press.

Bernstein, D. A. *et al.* (1994) *Psychology*, Boston: Houghton Mifflin.

Beutler, L. E. *et al.* (1986) 'Therapist variables in psychotherapy process and outcome', in S. L. Garfield and A. E. Bergin (eds), *Handbook of Psychotherapy and Behaviour Change*, Chichester: Wiley.

Bloch, S. and Chodoff, P. (1981) *Psychiatric Ethics*, Oxford: Oxford University Press.

Boker, W. (1992) 'A call for partnership between schizophrenic patients, relatives and professionals', *British Journal of Psychiatry* 161, 10–12.

Breggin, P. (1979) *Electroshock: its brain disabling effects*, NY: Springer.

Brown, G. W. and Harris, T. O. (1978) *Social origins of depression*, London: Tavistock.

Busfield, J. (1996) 'Professionals, the state and the development of mental health policy', in T. Heller *et al.* (eds), *Mental Health Matters*, London: Macmillan.

Cannon, D. S. *et al.* (1981) 'Emetic and electric shock alcohol aversion therapy: six and twelve month follow-up', *Journal of Consulting and Clinical Psychology* 49, 360–8.

Cautela, J. R. (1967) 'Covert sensitisation', *Psychology Reports* 20, 459–68.

Clark, D. (1966) 'Behaviour therapy of Gilles de la Tourettes syndrome' *British Journal of Psychiatry*, 112, 771–8.

Clark, D. (1993) 'Treating panic attacks', *The Psychologist* 6, 73–4.

Clipson, C. R. and Steer, J. M. (1998) *Case Studies In Abnormal Psychology*, Boston: Houghton Mifflin.

Cochrane. R. (1977) 'Mental illness in immigrants to England and Wales', *Social Psychiatry* 12, 25–35.

Cochrane, R. and Sashidharan, S. P. (1995) 'Mental health and ethnic minorities: a review of the literature and implications for services', paper presented to Birmingham and North Birmingham Health Trust.

Conners, C. (1980) *Food Additives and Hyperactive Children*, NY: Plenum Press.

Cooper, D. (1967) *Psychiatry and antipsychiatry*, London: Paladin.

Cooperstock, R. and Lennard, H. L. (1979) 'Some social meanings of tranquilliser use', *Sociology of Health and Illness* 1, 331–47.

Craske, M. and Barlow, D. (1993) 'Panic disorder and agoraphobia', in D. Barlow (ed.), *Clinical Handbook of Psychological Disorders: A step-by-step treatment manual*, NY: Guildford.

Crooks, R. L. and Stein, J. (1991) *Psychology: Science, Behaviour and Life*, London: Harcourt, Brace, Jovanovich.

Crow, T. J. *et al.* (1982) 'Two syndromes in schizophrenia and their pathogenesis', in F. A. Henn and G. A. Nasrallah (eds), *Schizophrenia as a Brain Disease*, NY: Oxford University Press.

Dallos, R. and Cullen, C (1990) 'Clinical psychology', in I. Roth (ed.), *Introduction to Psychology*, Hove: Erlbaum.

Davison, G. and Neale, J. (1990) *Abnormal Psychology*, NY: Wiley.

Dayson, D. (1993) 'The TAPS project 12: crime, vagrancy, death and readmission', *British Medical Journal* 162, 40–4.

Devine, P. and Fernald, P. (1973) 'Outcome effects of receiving a preferred, randomly assigned or non-preferred therapy', *Journal of Consulting and Clinical Psychology* 41(1) , 104–7.

Durham, R. *et al.* (1994) 'Cognitive therapy, analytic psychotherapy and anxiety management training for generalised anxiety disorder', *British Journal of Psychiatry* 165, 315–23.

Eastman, N. (1996) 'The need to change mental health law', in T. Heller *et al.* (eds), *Mental Health Matters*, London: Macmillan.

Edwards, J. (1995) 'Depression, antidepressants and accidents', *British Medical Journal* 311, 887–8.

Elkins, I. *et al.* (1989) 'NIMH treatment of depression collaborative research program', *Archives of General Psychiatry* 46, 971–82.

Ellis, A. (1962) *Reason and Emotion in Psychotherapy*, NJ: Citadel Press

Ellis, A. (1991) 'The revised ABC of rational-emotive therapy', *Journal of Rational Emotive and Cognitive Behaviour Therapy* 9, 139–92.

Erinosho, O. and Ayonrinde, A. (1981) 'Educational background and attitude to mental illness among the Yoruba in Nigeria', *Human Relations* 34, 1–12.

Evans, M. *et al.* (1992) 'Differential relapse following cognitive therapy and pharmacology for depression', *Archives of General Psychiatry* 49, 802–8.

Eysenck, H. J. (1952) 'The effects of psychotherapy: an evaluation', *Journal of Consulting Psychology* 16, 319–24.

Eysenck, H. J. (1965) 'The effects of psychotherapy', *International Journal of Psychiatry* 1, 7–142.

Feingold, B. (1975) *Why Your Child Is Hyperactive*, NY: Random House.

Fernando, S. (1988) *Race and Culture in Psychiatry*, London: Croom Helm.

Fox. P. *et al.* (1997) 'Cutting out stuttering', *New Scientist* (February), 32–5.

Frankl, V. (1959) *Man's Search for Meaning: An Introduction to Logotherapy*, Boston, MA: Beacon Press.

Fransella, F. (1990) 'Personal Construct Therapy', in W. Dryden (ed.), *Individual Therapy: A Handbook*, Milton Keynes: Oxford University Press.

Freud, A. (1952) 'The role of bodily illness in the mental life of children', *Psychoanalytic Study of the Child*, 7, International University Press.

Gabe, J. (1996) 'The History of Tranquilliser Use', in T. Heller (ed.) *Mental Health and Health Matters*, London: Macmillan.

Garrett, T. (1994) 'Epidemiology in the USA', in D. Jehu (ed.), *Patients as victims*, Chichester: Wiley.

Gittleman-Klein, R. *et al.* (1976) 'Relative efficacy of methylphenidate and behaviour modification in hyperkinetic children: an interim report', *Journal of Abnormal Child Psychology* 4, 361–79.

Goffman, E. (1961) *Asylums*, Middlesex: Pelican.

Gross, R. (1994) *Key Studies in Psychology*, Hodder & Stoughton.

Grant, P. (1994) 'Psychotherapy and race', in P. Clarkson and M. Pokorny (eds), *The Handbook of Psychotherapy*, London: Routledge.

Greist, J. *et al.* (1997) 'B. T. Steps', *New Scientist* (August), 26–31.

Gross, R. (1992) *Psychology: The Science of Mind and Behaviour*, London: Hodder and Stoughton.

Grunbaum, A. (1984) *The Foundations of Psychoanalysis: A Philosophical Critique*, Berkeley: University of California Press.

Gurman, A. S. *et al.* (1986) 'Research on the process and outcome of marital and family therapy', in S. Garfield and A Bergin (eds), *Handbook of Psychotherapy and Behaviour Change*, NY: Wiley.

Haaga, D. and Davison, G. (1993) 'An appraisal of rational-emotive therapy', *Journal of Consulting and Clinical Psychology* 61, 215–20.

Haddock, G. (1998) 'Psychological treatment of psychosis: current practice and future challenges', *The Psychologist* 11(6), 275–6.

Hamilton, S. *et al.* (1986) 'Sex bias, diagnosis and DSM III', *Sex Roles* 15, 269–74.

Harlow, J. M. (1868) *Recovery From the Passage of an Iron Bar Through the Head*, publication of the Massachusetts Medical Society, 2, 327 ff.

Hay. P. *et al.* (1993) 'Treatment of obsessive-compulsive disorder by psychosurgery', *Acta Psychiatrica Scandinavia* 87, 197–207.

Hazelrigg, M. *et al.* (1987) 'Evaluating the effectiveness of family therapies: an integrative review and analysis', *Psychological Bulletin* 101, 428–42.

Heather, N. (1976) *Radical Perspectives in Psychology*, London: Methuen.

Hock, R. (1992) *Forty Studies That Changed Psychology*, NJ: Prentice Hall.

Hogarty, G. E. *et al.* (1974) *Drug and sociotherapy in the aftercare of schizophrenic patients: II. Two-year relapse rates*, Archives of General Psychiatry 31, 603–8.

Hollon, S. *et al.* (1992) 'Cognitive therapy and pharmacotherapy for depression: singly and in combination', *Archives of General Psychiatry* 49, 774–81.

Howarth, I. (1989) 'Psychotherapy: who benefits?', *The Psychologist* 2(4), 150–2.

Hughes, J. R. and Pierattini, R. (1992) *An introduction to pharma-cotherapy*, in J. Grabowski and G. R. Vandenbos (eds),

Psychopharmacology: Basic Mechanisms and Applied Interventions: Master Lectures in Psychology, Washington D.C.: American Psychological Association.

Illich, I. (1975) *Medical Nemesis*, London: Calder & Boyars.

Irwin, M. *et al.* (1985) 'Psychotic patients' understanding of informed consent', *American Journal of Psychiatry* 165, 179–94.

Isaacs, W. *et al.* (1960) 'Application of operant conditioning to reinstate verbal behaviour in psychotics', *Journal of Speech and Hearing Disorders* 25, 8–12.

Jackson, D. and Weakland, J. (1961) 'Conjoint family therapy: Some considerations on theory, technique and results', *Psychiatry* 24, 30–45.

Jacobson, N. and Truax, P. (1991) 'Clinical significance: a statistical approach to defining meaningful change in psychotherapy research', *Journal of Consulting and Clinical Psychology* 59, 12–19.

Jakobi, S. and Pratt, D. (1992) 'Therapy notes and the law', *The Psychologist* (May), 219–21.

Jahoda, M. (1958) *Current Concepts of Positive Mental Health*, New York: Basic Books.

James, I. and Blackburn, I. (1995) 'Cognitive therapy with obsessive-compulsive disorder', *British Journal of Psychiatry* 166, 144–50.

Jones, L. and Cochrane, R. (1981) 'Stereotypes of mental illness: a test of the labelling hypothesis', *International Journal of Social Psychiatry* 27, 99–107.

Jones, M. C. (1925) 'A laboratory study of fear: the case of Peter', *Pedagogical Seminary* 31, 308–15.

Julien, R. M. (1992) *A Primer for Drug Action*, New York: W. H. Freeman.

Karasu, T. *et al.* (1979) 'Age factors in patient–therapist relationship', *Journal of Nervous and Mental Disorders* 167, 100–4.

Kelly, G. A. (1955) *A Theory of Personality – The Psychology of Personal Constructs*, NY: Norton.

Kirsch, I and Sapirstein, G. (1998) In M. Day, 'Mostly in the mind', *New Scientist* 2412, 13.

Klein, M. (1932) *The Psychoanalysis of Children*, London: Hogarth.

Klosko, J. S. *et al.* (1990) 'A comparison of alprazolam and behaviour therapy in treatment of panic disorder', *Journal of Consulting and Clinical Psychology* 58, 77–84.

Koss, M. and Butcher, J. (1986) 'Research on brief psychotherapy', in S. Bergin and A. Garfield (eds), *Handbook of Psychotherapy and Behaviour Change*, NY: Wiley.

Laing, R. D. (1965) *The Divided Self*, Middlesex: Penguin.

Lambert, M. *et al.* (1986) 'The effectiveness of psychotherapy', in S. Garfield and A. Bergin (eds), *Handbook of Psychotherapy and Behaviour Change*, NY: Wiley.

Lang, P. and Melamed, B. (1969) 'Case report: avoidance conditioning therapy of an infant with chronic ruminative vomiting', *Journal of Abnormal Psychology* 74, 1–8.

Leonard, H. *et al.* (1989) 'Treatment of obsessive-compulsive disorder with clomipramine and desipramine in children and adolescents: a double-blind crossover comparison', *Archives of General Psychiatry* 46, 1088–92.

Lickey, M. E. and Gordon, B. (1991) *Medicine and Mental Illness: the Use of Drugs in Mental Illness*, New York: W. H. Freeman & Co.

Lidz, C. *et al.* (1993) 'The accuracy of predictions of violence to others', *Journal of the American Medical Association* 269, 1007–11.

Lindsay, G. and Colley, A. (1995) 'Ethical dilemmas of members of the society', *The Psychologist* (October), 448–51.

Linn, K. *et al.* (1991) 'Ethnicity and family involvement in the treatment of schizophrenic patients', *Journal of Nervous and Mental Disorders* 179, 631–3.

Lovaas, O. (1977) *The Autistic Child: Language Development Through Behaviour Modification*, NY: Irvington.

Luborsky, L and Spence, D. (1978) 'Quantitative research on psycho-analytic therapy', in S. Garfield and A. Bergin (eds), *Handbook of Psychotherapy and Behaviour Change*, NY: Wiley.

King, M. *et al.* (1990) 'Long term use of benzodiazepines: the views of patients', *British Journal of General Practice* 40: 194–6.

Mair, K. (1997) 'Psychological treatment for Dissociative Identity Disorder: risks and benefits', paper given at BPS conference, London, 17 December.

Malan, D. *et al.* (1975) 'Psychodynamic changes in untreated neurotic patients', *Archives of General Psychiatry* 32, 110–26.

Malleson, A. (1973) *Need Your Doctor Be So Useless?* London: George, Allen & Unwin.

Marcus (1985) 'Freud and Dora: Story, History, Case History', in C. Bernheimer and C. Kahane (eds) *In Dora's Case: Freud-Hysteria-Feminism*, NY: Columbia University Press.

Marks, I. (1970) cited in R. D. Gross (1992) *Psychology: The Science of Mind and Behaviour*, London: Hodder & Stoughton.

Marks, I. (1981) *Care and Cure of Neuroses: Theory and Practice of Behavioural Psychotherapy*, New York: Wiley.

Marks, I. (1987) *Fears, Phobias and Rituals*, New York: Oxford University Press.

Marks, I. and O'Sullivan, G. (1988) 'Drugs and psychological treatments for agoraphobia/panic and obsessive-compulsive disorders: a review', *British Journal of Psychiatry* 153, 650–8.

Martin, J. (1985) *Hospitals in Trouble*, Oxford: Blackwell.

Maslow, A. (1954) *Motivation and Personality*, NY: Harper & Row.

Masson, J. (1988) *Against Therapy*, London: Collins

May, P. (1975) 'A follow-up study of the treatment of schizophrenia', in R. Spitzer and D. Klein (eds) *Evaluation of Psychological Therapies*, Baltimore: Johns Hopkins University Press.

McCord, J. (1978) 'A thirty year follow up of treatment effects', *American Psychologist* (March), 284–9.

McGrath, T. *et al.* (1990) 'Successful treatment of a noise phobia in a nine year-old girl with systematic desensitisation in vivo', *Educational Psychologist* 10(1), 79–83.

Meichenbaum, D. (1976) 'Towards a cognitive therapy of self-control', in G. Schwartz and D. Shapiro (eds), *Consciousness and Self-Regulation: Advances in Research*, NY: Plenum.

Meltzer, D. *et al.* (1991) 'Community care for patients with schizophrenia one year after hospital discharge', *British Medical Journal* 303, 1023–6.

Menzies, R. and Clarke, J. (1993) 'A comparison of in vivo and vicarious exposure in the treatment of childhood water phobia', *Behaviour Research and Therapy* 31(1), 9–15.

Miller, R. and Berman, J. (1983) 'The efficacy of cognitive-behaviour therapies: a quantitative review of the research evidence', *Psychological Bulletin* 94, 39–53.

Mitchell, K. M. (1977) 'A reappraisal of the therapeutic effectiveness of accurate empathy, nonpossessive warmth and genuineness', in A. Gurman and A. Razin (eds), *Effective Psychotherapy: a Handbook of Research*, NY: Pergamon.

Moorey, S. (1990) 'Cognitive therapy', in W. Dryden (ed.), *Individual Therapy: A Handbook*, Milton Keynes: Oxford University Press.

Mowrer, O. (1947) 'On the dual nature of learning', *Harvard Educational Review* 17, 102–48.

Mowrer, O. and Mowrer, W. (1938) 'Enuresis: a method for its study and treatment', *American Journal of Orthopsychiatry* 8, 436–59.

Muijen, M. (1996) 'Scare in the community: Britain in moral panic', in T. Heller *et al.* (eds), *Mental Health Matters*, London: Macmillan.

Muijen, M. *et al* (1994) 'Community psychiatric nurse teams: intensive support versus generic care', *British Journal of Psychiatry*, 165, 179–94.

NIMH (1987) 'The switch process in manic-depressive illness', DHHS publication no. ADM 81–108, Washington, DC: Goverment Printing Office.

Okocha, C. (1998) 'Current management of anxiety disorders', *The Practitioner* 242, 39–46.

Orford, J. (1963) *The Social Psychology of Mental Disorder*, Penguin Education.

Orlinsky, D. and Howard, K. (1987) 'A generic model of psychotherapy', *Journal of Integrative and Eclectic Psychotherapy* 6, 6–27.

Parloff, M. *et al.* (1978) 'Research on therapist variables in relation to process and outcome', in S. Garfield and A. Bergin (eds), *Handbook of Psychotherapy and Behaviour Change*, NY: Wiley.

Parry, G. (1996) 'Using research to change practice', in T. Heller *et al.* (eds), *Mental Health Matters*, London: Macmillan.

Parsons, T. (1951) *The Social System*, Glencoe, IL: Free press.

Paul, G. (1967) 'Insight versus desensitisation in psychotherapy two years after termination', *Journal of Consulting Psychology* 31, 333–48.

Perls, F. (1969) *Gestalt Therapy Verbatim*, NY: Bantam.

Piccinelli, M. *et al.* (1995) 'Efficacy of drug treatment in obsessive-compulsive disorder: a meta-analytic review', *British Journal of Psychiatry* 166, 424–33.

Pilgrim, D. and Rogers, A. (1996) 'Two notions of risk in mental health debates', in T. Heller *et al.* (eds), *Mental Health Matters*, London: Macmillan.

Prien, R. *et al*. (1984) 'Drug therapy in the prevention of recurrences in unipolar and bipolar affective disorders', *Archives of General Psychiatry* 41, 1096–104.

Prioleau, L. *et al*. (1983) 'An analysis of psychotherapy versus placebo studies', *Behaviour and Brain Sciences* 6, 273–310.

Rachman, S. and Hodgson, R. (1980) *Obsessions and Compulsions*, Englewood Cliffs, NJ: Prentice Hall.

Reich, W. (1981) 'Psychiatric diagnosis as an ethical problem', in S. Bloch and P. Chodoff, *Psychiatric Ethics*, Oxford: Oxford University Press.

Richardson, J. *et al*. (1994) 'Verbal learning by major depressive disorder patients during treatment with fluoxetine or amitriptyline', *International Clinical Psychopharmacology* 9, 35–40.

Robins, L. *et al*. (1984) 'Lifetime prevalence of specific psychiatric disorders in three sites', *Archives of General Psychiatry*, 41, 942–9.

Rogers, A. (1993) 'Coercion and voluntary admission: an examination of psychiatric patient views', *Behavioural Sciences and the Law*, 11, 258–67.

Rogers, C. (1951) *Client-Centered Therapy – Its Current Practices, Implications and Theory*, Boston, MA: Houghton Mifflin.

Rogers, C. (1970) *Carl Rogers on Encounter Groups*, New York: Harper & Row.

Rogers, C. (1980) *A Way of Being*, Boston, MA: Houghton Mifflin.

Rose, G and Marshall, T. (1974) *Counselling and School Social Work: An Experimental Study*, London: Wiley.

Rosenbluth, D. (1974) 'Psychotherapy with the pre-schoolchild: a psychoanalytic approach', in V. Varma (ed.) *Psychotherapy Today*, London: Constable.

Rosenhan, D.L. and Seligman (1984) *Abnormal Psychology*, New York: W.W. Norton.

Rosman, B. *et al*. (1976) 'Input and outcome of family therapy of anorexia nervosa', in J. L. Claghom (ed.) *Successful psychotherapy*, New York: Basic Books.

Rosser, R. *et al*. (1987) 'Five year follow-up of patients treated with in-patient psychotherapy at the Cassel Hospital for Nervous Disorders', *Journal of the Royal Society of Medicine* 80, 549–55.

Roth, A. and Fonagy, P. (1996) *What Works For Whom? A Critical Review of Psychotherapy Research*, NY: Guilford Press.

171

Rush, A. *et al.* (1977) 'Comparative efficacy of cognitive therapy and pharmacotherapy in the treatment of depressed patients', *Cognitive Therapy and Research* 1, 17–39.

Sackheim, H. (1988) 'The efficacy of electroconvulsive therapy', *Annals of the New York Academy of Science* 462, 70–5.

Sackheim, H. A. *et al.* (1993) 'Effects of Stimulus Intensity and Electrode Replacement on the Efficacy of the Effects of Electroconvulsive Therapy', *New England Journal of Medicine* 328, 839–46.

Sedgwick, P. (1982) *Psychopolitics*, London: Pluto.

Seligman, M. (1975) *Helplessness: On Depression, Development and Death*, San Francisco: W.H. Freeman.

Shapiro, D. (1990) 'Recent applications of meta-analysis in clinical research', *Clinical Psychology Review* 5, 13–34.

Shapiro, D. A. and Shapiro, D. (1982) 'Meta-analysis of comparative therapy outcome studies: a replication and refinement', *Psychological Bulletin* 92, 581–604.

Shapiro, M. (1985) 'A reassessment of clinical psychology as an applied science', *British Journal of Clinical Psychology* 24(1), 1–13

Skinner, B. F. (1938) *Science and Behaviour*, NY: Macmillan.

Sloane, R. *et al.* (1975) *Psychotherapy versus Behaviour Therapy*, Cambridge, MA: Harvard University Press.

Smail, D. (1987) *Taking Care: An Alternative To Therapy*, London: Dent.

Smail, D. (1991) 'Towards a radical environmentalist psychology of help', *The Psychologist* 2, 61–5.

Smail, D. (1996) 'Psychotherapy and Tragedy', *Psychotherapy Section Newsletter* 20, 3–13.

Smith, M. *et al.* (1980) *The Benefits Of Psychotherapy*, Baltimore: Johns Hopkins University Press.

Snaith, R.P. (1994) 'Psychosurgery: Controversy and Enquiry', *British Journal of Psychotherapy* 161, 582–4.

Solomon, R. and Wynne, L. (1954) 'Traumatic avoidance learning: the principle of anxiety conservation and partial irreversibility', *Psychology Review* 81, 353–85.

Steiner, W. (1991) 'Fluoxetine-induced mania in a patient with obsessive-compulsive disorder', *American Journal of Psychiatry*, 148, 1403–4.

Stiles, W. *et al.* (1986) 'Are all psychotherapies equivalent?', *American Psychology* 41, 165–80.

Strupp, H. H. (1993) 'The Vanderbilt psychotherapy studies: synopsis', *Journal of Consulting and Clinical Psychology* 61, 431–3.

Sue, D. (1990) 'Culture-specific strategies in counselling: a conceptual framework', *Professional Psychology: Research and Practice* 21, 424–33.

Suppes, T. *et al.* (1991) 'Risk of recurrence following discontinuation of lithium treatment in bipolar disorder', *Archives of General Psychiatry* 48, 1082–7.

Stuart, R. (1976) 'An operant interpersonal program for couples', in D. H. L. Olson (ed.) *Treating Relationships*, Lake Mills, IA: Graphic Publishing Company.

Svartburg, M. and Stiles, T. (1991) 'Comparative effects of short-term psychodynamic psychotherapy: a meta-analysis', *Journal of Consulting and Clinical Psychology* 59(5), 704–14.

Szasz, T. S. (1962) *The Myth of Mental Illness*, NY: Harper & Row.

Szasz, T. S. (1974) *Ideology and Insanity*, Harmondsworth: Penguin.

Tate, B. and Baroff, G. (1966) 'Aversive control of self-injurious behaviour in a psychotic boy', *Behaviour Research and Therapy* 4, 281–7.

Taylor, D. (1987) 'Current usage of benzodiazepines in Great Britain', in H. Freeman and Y. Rue (eds) *Benzodiazepines in Current Clinical Practice*, London: Royal Society of Medicine Services.

Teasdale, J. (1997) 'Understanding and preventing depression', paper presented at BPS Annual Conference, 5th April 1997.

Thigpen, C. H. and Cleckley, H. (1954) 'A case of multiple personality', *The Journal of Abnormal and Social Psychology*, 49, 135–51.

Tinkelpaugh, O. (1928) 'An experimental study of representative factors in monkeys', *Journal of Comparative Psychology* 8, 197–236.

Truax, C. (1996) 'Reinforcement and non-reinforcement in Rogerian therapy', *Journal of Abnormal Psychology*, 71, 1–9.

Truax, C, and Carkhuff, R. (1964) 'Significant developments in psychotherapy research', in L. Abt and B. Reiss (eds), *Progress in Clinical Psychology*, NY: Grune & Stratton.

Tyrer, P. and Steinberg, D. (1987) *Models for Mental Disorder*, London: Wiley.

UKAN (1995) 'UKAN's national user survey', *Open Mind* 78, 11–14.

van Deurzen-Smith, E. (1990) 'Existential Therapy', in W. Dryden (ed.) *Individual Therapy: A Handbook*, Milton Keynes: Oxford University.

Wallerstein, R. (1989) 'The psychotherapy research project of the Menninger Foundation: an overview', *Journal of Consulting and Clinical Psychology* 57, 195–205.

Wallerstein, R. (1957) *Hospital Treatment of Alcoholism: A Comparative Experimental Study*, New York: Basic Books.

Watson, J. and Rayner, R. (1920) 'Conditioned emotional responses', *Journal of Experimental Psychology* 3, 1–14.

Wehr, T. and Rosenthal, N. (1989) 'Seasonability and affective illness', *American Journal of Psychiatry* 146, 201–4.

Wilson, G. and Rachman. S. (1983) 'Meta-analysis and the evaluations of psychotherapy outcome: limitations and liabilities', *Journal of Consulting and Clinical Psychology* 51, 54–64.

Wittman, W. and Matt. G. (1986) 'Meta-analysis as a method for integrating psychotherapeutic studies in German-speaking countries', *Psychologische Rundschau* 37, 20–40.

Wolpe, J. (1958) *Psychotherapy by Reciprocal Inhibition*, Stanford, CA: Stanford University Press.

Wolpe, J. (1973) *The Practice of Behaviour Therapy*, NY: Pergamon.

Worell, J. and Remer, P. (1992) *Feminist Perspectives in Therapy*, Chichester: Wiley.

Yalom, I. (1980) *Existential Psychotherapy*, New York: Basic books.

Yates, A. (1958) 'The application of learning theory to the treatment of tics', *Journal of Abnormal and Social Psychology* 56, 175–82.

Zigler, E. and Phillips, L. (1961) 'Psychiatric diagnosis and symptomatology', *Journal of Abnormal Psychology* 63, 69–75.

Index